THE GREAT WALL

History and Pictures

FOREIGN LANGUAGES PRESS   BEIJING

First Edition 1995

Editor: Yan Qiubai
Design: Li Shiji
Text: Luo Zhewen and Yan Qiubai
Translation: Arnold Chao
Photographs: Bai Songyan, Bai Liang, Cai Haifeng, Cheng Dongyin, Chen Hao, Chen Shubo, Dong Ruicheng, Gao Bo, Gao Cunrui, Guo Changqing, Guo Xian, Gu Wei, Han Dezhou, Han Sandang, He Ke, Hu Dunzhi, Huo Jianying, Jiang Jingyu, Jiang Jiping, Liu Chungen, Liu Shizhao, Liu Wenmin, Lu Zhongmin, Luo Zhewen, Meng Zi, Qu Weibo, Ren Yinen, Sun Shuming, Sun Yongxue, Tian Chunyu, Wang Deying, Wang Jingui, Wang Zhengbao, Xu Yishan, Wei Mingxiang, Yan Xinqiang, Yu Yuntian, Zhai Xinjian, Zhou Youma and Zong Tongchang

ISBN 7 – 119 – 01464 – 1

© Foreign Languages Press, Beijing, China, 1995

Published by Foreign Languages Press
24 Baiwanzhaung Road, Beijing 100037, China

Distributed by China International Book Trading Corporation
35 Chegongzhuang Xilu, Beijing 100044, China
P.O. Box 399, Beijing, China

Printed in the People's Republic of China

万里长城

严秋白　编

＊

ⓒ外文出版社

（中国北京百万庄路 24 号）

邮政编码 100037

北京外文印刷厂印刷

中国国际图书贸易总公司发行

（中国北京车公庄西路 35 号）

北京邮政信箱第 399 号　邮政编码 100044

1995 年(12 开)第一版

（英）

ISBN 7 – 119 – 01464 – 1 /J·1266(外)

07500(平)

85 – E – 449P

CONTENTS

Magnificent.

Precipitous.

Mysterious.

Ancient.

The Great Wall Monument of China's History

Luo Zhewen

WHEN an astronaut lands on the moon and looks down on earth, one of the objects he can identify is the Great Wall of China. This colossal structure, which snakes over the undulating terrain of northern China, is comparable to any other historic wonder of the world in significance and magnificence.

Tens of millions of people built the wall over a period of more than 2,000 years, a project which speaks for the wisdom and tenacity of the builders and the level reached by China's traditional architecture. The wall we see today, dating basically from the Ming Dynasty (1368-1644), is the culmination of these centuries-long efforts, during which walls totalling 50,000 kilometres were built for national defence. If the earth, stones and bricks making up the Ming wall were used to erect a smaller wall one metre thick and five metres high, it could easily circle the earth. And if the same materials were used to build a road five metres wide and 35 centimetres deep, that road could circle the earth four times.

Construction of the Great Wall started in the 7th century B.C. during the Spring and Autumn period and ended in the middle of the 17th century when the Ming Dynasty went into decline. The work under the various dynasties included either joining up and reinforcing the old sections or adding new ones, with the result that an enormous dragon-like structure now appears to slither its way across the mountains and valleys of northern China.

Luo Zhewen, born in 1925, is a native of Yibin, Sichuan Province. A specialist in China's ancient architecture, he is a member of the Commission of Science and Technology under the Ministry of Culture, Vice-Chairman of the Committee for Historical and Theoretical Studies of the Chinese Society of Architecture, and Vice-President of the Chinese Society for the Study of the Great Wall. His works include *The Great Wall* and *A Concise History of China's Ancient Architecture*. Two more works, *Ancient Pagodas in China* and *China's Imperial Tombs and Mausoleums*, will soon be published by the Foreign Languages Press.

Aerial photo of the Great Wall taken with a remote sensor.

The wall has stood through times of peace between the Han Chinese who inhabited the Central Plains and the ethnic groups who lived in areas to the north as well as times of fierce hostilities between them. It has witnessed a succession of dynasties through some of history's bitterest struggles. The story of the Great Wall is a panorama of Chinese history, a record of the vicissitudes of the Chinese nation.

The Wall Before and During the Time of the First Emperor of Qin (7th century-209 B.C.)

It is generally thought that the Great Wall was built under the First Emperor of the Qin Dynasty (221-207 B.C.). Actually, construction of various sections of the wall started long before his time—back in the 7th century B.C. During the Spring and Autumn period (770-476 B.C.) and the period of the Warring States (475-221 B.C.), China was divided among a great number of ducal states under the nominal, powerless central dynasty of the Eastern Zhou (770-256 B.C.). Seven of the ducal states—the Qin, Qi, Chu, Han, Zhao, Wei and Yan —emerged as the strongest. While these states fought among themselves and built defence walls against one another, three of them—the Qin, Zhao and Yan—had to cope with yet another enemy which threatened them from the north—the Xiongnu (the Huns). Members of the nomadic Xiongnu tribes were good horse-riders and archers. With this powerful cavalry, the Xiongnu slave-owners launched frequent forays into the border areas of the Qin, Zhao and Yan and returned with captives, draught animals and valuables. This

The wall built in the time of the First Emperor of the Qin Dynasty.

The wall of the Western Han Dynasty (206 B.C.-A.D. 24). The earth on the surface has fallen off, revealing the inside.

The wall of the Sui Dynasty (581-618).

The wall of the Jurchen Dynasty (1115-1234), lined with a "boundary ditch" for its protection. To build the wall the conscripted labourers first dug a ditch and then used the earth thus excavated. (Top right)

The Cloud Terrace at Juyong Pass near Beijing. It was built over the road in 1342 with an arched gate by which chariots, horses and pedestrians could pass through. There used to be a row of three Tibetan-style Buddhist pagodas on the terrace —according to Buddhist scriptures, one could pay tribute to Buddha by walking beside a pagoda.

compelled the three states to build walls as defence barriers along their northern borders and station troops there. This was the beginning of the Great Wall.

Relying on his military superiority, the First Emperor of Qin had conquered all six rival states by 221 B.C. and then founded China's first centralized empire. Having established his authority across the Central Plains, the emperor sent General Meng Tian against the Xiongnu. With 300,000 troops, the general defeated the Xiongnu cavalry and recovered the entire Yellow River Bend. To reinforce the frontier defences against the Xiongnu, the First Emperor gave orders to launch an enormous project—the building of the Great Wall. The walls originally built in the states of the Qin, Zhao and Yan were joined up and extended to form a wall of more than 5,000 kilometres. These new sections together equalled more than half of the total of the old ones. Cutting across the north of China, the wall started in east Liaoning on the east and terminated in Min County, Gansu Province, on the west.

The wall made it possible to safeguard the lives and property of the people in northern China and to

ensure farm production and livestock raising in the border areas. But its construction meant a heavy burden for the people. Hundreds of thousands of men, and even some women, had to perform backbreaking labour at the construction sites, and tens of thousands of them lost their lives—including conscripted soldiers, slaves, convicts and ordinary people. The story of the Great Wall is inevitably associated with the tyranny of the First Emperor of Qin, who is both credited with his historical achievements and criticized for the sufferings he caused to the people.

The Wall After the Qin Dynasty (206 B.C.-A.D. 1368)

The fall of the Qin Dynasty was followed by the founding of the Western Han Dynasty in 206 B.C. The Xiongnu grew strong again and frequently invaded the Han empire.

While the new regime was first consolidating its power, it was unable to repel the Xiongnu attacks. Therefore it had to appease the raiders by sending them enormous amounts of expensive gifts every year, though even this did not stop the advance. It was not until the reign of Emperor Wu (140-87 B.C.) that the Han court, after having kept to a policy of economic recuperation for several decades, launched powerful counterattacks against the Xiongnu and drove them north of the Great Desert in Mongolia. Then the court started a major renovation of the Qin wall along the Yellow River, extending it to the far west. Passing Jiuquan and Dunhuang in Gansu, the Han Great Wall reached into present-day Xinjiang, then known as part of the "Western Regions." Fortified castles were erected along the wall and troops were stationed there. All through the first century of the Christian era tremendous amounts of manpower were invested

in the building of forts and beacon towers in today's Shaanxi, Shanxi and Hebei. Standing five kilometres apart, these installations formed a defence line inside the wall. Afterwards the Xiongnu tribes split up into a northern and a southern faction. As the latter pledged allegiance to the court of Han, hostilities came to a stop along the borders and no further major renovation of the Great Wall was necessary.

A confrontation between North and South China lasted for some 170 years from the beginning of the 5th century to the close of the 6th century. The dynasties which dominated the northern parts of China, including the Northern Wei (386-534), Eastern Wei (534-550), Northern Qi (550-577) and Northern Zhou (557-581), were all harassed by nomadic peoples living further to the north known as the Tujue and Rourang. Though limited in their resources, these regimes had to follow the practices of their predecessors

The Great Wall built under the Ming Dynasty (1368-1644) remains in good shape today, and certain sections look beautiful. Each section was designed according to the local topography. The sections in Beijing, Tianjin and Hebei show an ingenious use of strategic positions. (Left)

The Ming Great Wall winds its way along mountain ridges like a huge dragon.

by rebuilding the Great Wall. Large projects were carried out under the Northern Wei and Northern Qi. In 423 a 1,000-kilometre section of the wall, starting at Chicheng County, Hebei Province, on the east and terminating in the Urad banner in the present-day Inner Mongolia Autonomous Region on the west, was completed under the Northern Wei. Still bigger projects were undertaken by the Northern Qi, for example, from 550 to 559. In this period frontier posts, 15 kilometres apart, were built along a distance of 1,500 kilometres from northwest of Datong in Shanxi Province to the coast of the Bohai Sea. Also, a parallel wall was erected inside the Great Wall, starting at Pian Pass in Shanxi, passing through the Yanmen and Juyong passes, and reaching to north of Huairou County in today's municipality of Beijing.

The founding of the Sui Dynasty in 581 put an end to the division between North and South China and once again unified the Central Plains. The court of Sui, which lasted only 37 years, carried out as many as seven projects for renovation of the Great Wall in order to resist incursions by nomadic tribes like the Tujue, Qidan (Khitan) and Tuguhun. In 583 Emperor Wen built Yu Pass along the shore of the Bohai Sea. This is known as the Shanhai Pass today.

No major renovations were car-ried out during the Tang (618-907) and Song (960-1279) dynasties, except that fortified castles and towns were built along the borders for defence. Then, in the middle Song period there began rampant political corruption and a sharp decline in national strength. Taking advantage of this, the nomadic invaders under the dynasties of Liao (916-1125) and Jurchen (1115-1234) successively breached through the Great Wall and occupied parts of the Central Plains. The rulers of both the Liao and Jurchen were aware of the importance of the Great Wall and reinforced it as a barrier against the Mongols threatening them from the northern grasslands. With a length

The main castle of each pass along the Great Wall may take a simple or complex structure, depending on the geographical position and terrain. Shanhai Pass along the Bohai Sea coast consists of a number of walls and towers. This picture shows the 10-metre-wide top surface of the eastern gate, on which are mounted three towers.

A moat protects the walls of Shanhai Pass.

A platform on top of the Great Wall usually has battlements slightly higher than the wall itself.

A watchtower is generally two-storeyed. It is mounted on an elevated part of the wall and provided with holes for sighting and shooting at the enemy.

of 5,000 kilometres, the Jurchen version of the Great Wall was a significant achievement as compared with the walls rebuilt under other dynasties. In the 13th century, however, mounted Mongol troops started driving towards Beijing, then serving as the Zhongdu (Middle Capital) of the Jurchens. In a panic, the Jurchen rulers had the gates of Juyong Pass north of Beijing sealed with molten iron and sent their crack troops there. But the Mongols hired guides who knew every stone in the area and found a mountain trail which could accommodate a single mounted soldier at a time. So they bypassed Juyong Pass and the other military strongholds and crossed onto the North China plain without alarming the Jurchens.

Having taken Beijing, the Mongols renamed it Dadu (Great Capital). The Yuan Dynasty was then founded by them in 1271. As they were the very people who had come from the northern grasslands, they faced no threat from that direction and saw no need to rebuild the Great Wall. However, they did renovate some of the passes along the wall. For instance, the Yuntai (Cloud Terrace) inside Juyong Pass, which has a strong religious flavour, is a legacy of the Yuan Dynasty.

The Ming Great Wall (1368-1644)

After the Mongolian nobility enjoyed power and luxury in Beijing for almost 100 years, its rule was shaken by peasant insurrections in southern China, leading to the founding of the Ming Dynasty in 1368. As the Ming troops stormed the city of Beijing, the Mongolian nobles fled to their homeland on the pastures north of the Great Desert. But they were not resigned in their defeat and made incursions into Ming territory in the hope of restoring their rule. Meanwhile, the Jurchens in Northeast China had rebuilt their strength and presented a serious menace to the Ming empire. Like their predecessors, the Ming rulers considered a powerful Great Wall almost the only means of resisting the nomadic invaders. Indeed, reconstruction of the wall never stopped for the more than 200 years during the Ming period. The project was conducted on a gigantic scale, and improvements in engineering technology made the wall an impregnable barrier by the

military standards of the time. Historians share the opinion that the Great Wall was finally completed under the Ming.

Ming emperors consistently appointed their trusted ministers to be supervisors of the wall project, and some of the emperors went to inspect the construction sites. For example, the famous general, Xu Da, was sent to build Juyong Pass, Gubeikou Pass and other strongholds at the very beginning of the dynasty. The Ming wall was basically completed in about 100 years. It covered some 7,300 kilometres, stretching from the Yalu River on the east to Jiayu Pass on the west. The section from the Yalu River to Shanhai Pass, however, which had a length of almost 1,000 kilometres, was built of stone and earth and was not as well constructed as some other sec-

tions. Today it has become largely dilapidated or even untraceable. This has given rise to the common misconception that Shanhai Pass is the eastern end of the Great Wall.

For effective defence along the northern frontiers, the Ming authorities divided the entire Great Wall belt into nine zones and placed each under the control of a *zhen* (garrison headquarters)—hence the Ming term of "the important garrison headquarters in the nine defence

zones." Two more garrison headquarters were added later, one for the defence of Beijing and the other for the protection of the imperial tombs at Changping northwest of Beijing. Thus the defence system consisted of eleven garrisons in nine zones. These were:

Liaodong Garrison: Based in today's Liaoyang, Liaoning Province, and responsible for some 1,000 kilometres of the Great Wall from the banks of the Yalu River to Shanhai Pass.

Ji Garrison: Based in today's Qianxi, Hebei Province, and responsible for some 880 kilometres of the wall from Shanhai Pass to Mutianyu. This was a solidly built, and perhaps the most magnificent and beautiful section of the wall.

Chang Garrison: Based in Changping, northwest of Beijing,

and responsible for a 230-kilometre section of the wall from Mutianyu on the east to Zijing Pass on the west. It was particularly for the defence of the capital and the imperial tombs.

Zhenbao Garrison: Based in Baoding, Hebei Province, and responsible for a 390-kilometre section of the wall from Zijing Pass on the north to Gu Pass on the south. It was established to strengthen defences in the southwestern neighbourhood of the capital.

Xuanfu Garrison: Based in Xuanhua, Hebei Province, and responsible for a 510-kilometre section of the wall from Juyong Pass to northeast of Datong, Shanxi Province. Since the garrison controlled the northwest gateway to Beijing, as many as nine walls were built along this section, one behind the other,

The second storey of a watchtower is surrounded with walls which have windows and holes for the shooting of arrows and other projectiles.

This three-storeyed watchtower is a rare one on the Great Wall. It is located on a hill of Jinshanling in Miyun County, Beijing.

Bedrooms for the guards are found on the second floors of many watchtowers. (Bottom)

Map

Dunhuang

Jiayu Pass Jiuquan

Zhangye

W

the Great Wall

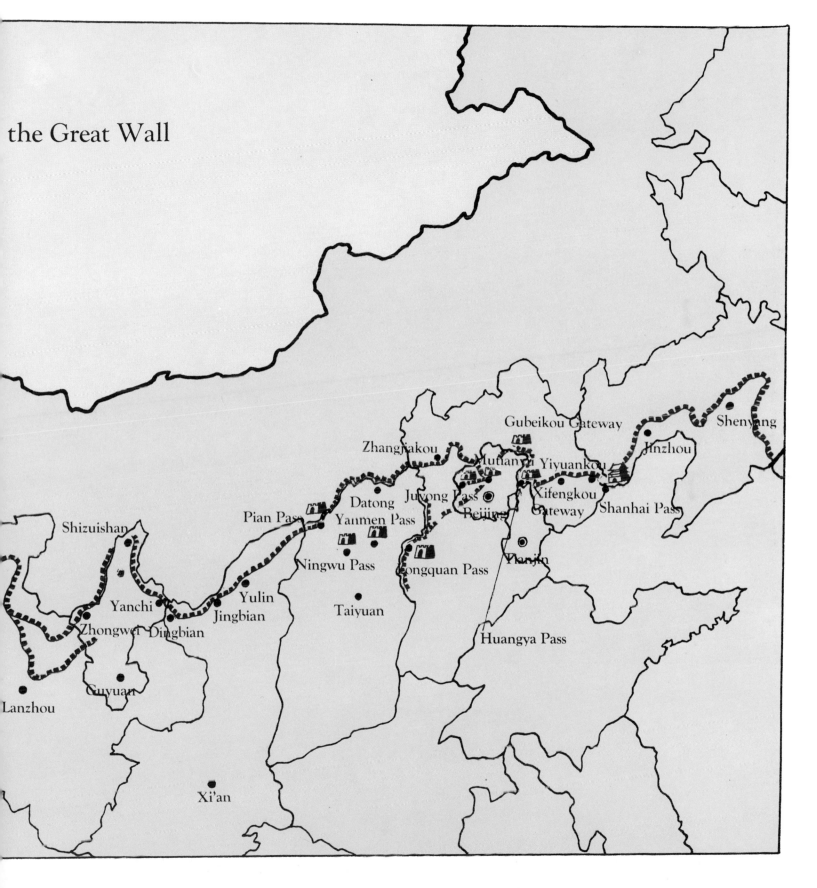

Gubeikou Gateway

Shenyang

Zhangjiakou

Jinzhou

Mutianyu Yiyuankou

Juyong Pass

Xifengkou
Gateway

Shanhai Pass

Datong

Beijing

Pian Pass

Yanmen Pass

Shizuishan

Ningwu Pass

Longquan Pass

Tianjin

Yulin

Yanchi

Jingbian

Taiyuan

Zhongwei Dingbian

Huangya Pass

Guyuan

Lanzhou

Xi'an

The interiors of watchtowers vary from place to place.

A staircase between the upper and lower floors inside a watchtower. It is only wide enough for one person at a time.

each guarded by a large number of troops.

Datong Garrison: Based in Datong, Shanxi Province, and responsible for a 350-kilometre section of the wall from Tianzhen, Shanxi, on the east to Pian Pass near the Yellow River on the west.

Shanxi Garrison (also called **Taiyuan Garrison**): Based in Pian Pass and responsible for some 800 kilometres of the wall along the border between Shanxi and Hebei and within Shanxi. This section of the wall started at Huangyuling near Heshun in southeastern Shanxi, went north to Longquan Pass, turned west to travel through four more passes—Pingxing, Yanmen, Ningwu and Pian—and finally reached Baode on the banks of the Yellow River in the south. Located to the south of the garrisons of Datong and Xuanfu, the section of the wall controlled by the Shanxi Garrison was called the "Inner Great Wall."

Yansui Garrison (also called **Yu-lin Garrison**): Based in Yulin, Shaanxi Province, and responsible for an 880-kilometre section of the wall from Fugu, Shaanxi, on the east to Yanchi, Ningxia, on the west.

Ningxia Garrison: Based in Yinchuan, Ningxia, and responsible for a 1,000-kilometre section of the wall from Yanchi, Ningxia, on the east to Lanzhou, Gansu, on the west.

Guyuan Garrison: Based in Guyuan, Ningxia, and responsible for a 500-kilometre section of the wall from Jingbian, Shaanxi, on the east to Gaolan, Gansu, on the west. It was contiguous to the Yansui (Yulin) Garrison on the east and to the Gansu Garrison on the west.

Gansu Garrison: Based in Zhangye, Gansu, and responsible for an 800-kilometre section of the wall from Lanzhou, Gansu, on the east to Jiayu Pass on the west.

In addition to establishing the eleven garrisons in the nine zones listed above, the Ming government built some 1,000 fortified towns and castles along the Great Wall. The bigger ones were called *guan* (pass), and the smaller ones, *kou* (post). They were usually erected on precipitous terrain, true to the saying that "one man operating from a commanding height can hold off ten thousand soldiers below." Both sides of the Great Wall were lined with garrison posts and beacon towers for communication of military information. Thus the Ming authorities completed a close-knit system of military defences along the Great Wall. The Ming wall also surpassed previous versions of the wall in engineering quality. For example, most sections of the wall have survived the wind and rain of the past 600 years and remain intact on hilltops, in mountain valleys, on the grasslands or in the deserts and today still impress the Chinese as well as foreign visitors with their dignified look.

The Defence System and Construction Methods

The Great Wall was built primarily as a defence structure. For some 2,000 years during China's feudal times, a countless number of big and small wars took place on both sides of the wall. By nature these were wars fought between China's different ethnic groups. Whether the country was ruled by the Hans or by one of the ethnic minorities which had gained control of the Central Plains, the government spared no money or manpower to build or rebuild the Great Wall, using the insurmountable barriers, deep moats and fortified castles of the wall to defend itself. Understandably, such a defence strategy did serve to protect the country and the life of its people in the days when the weaponry consisted of swords and spears, lances and halberds, and bows and arrows. But as the economy developed and changes took place in military strategies and tactics, improvements had to be made in both the design and construction technology of the Great Wall. In particular, the Ming period saw the creation of a sophisticated defence system along the wall embracing garrison towns, garrison posts, passes, blockhouses, additional wall structures, watchtowers and beacon towers, each given a different status and designed mission. The system enabled the central government to stay in touch with military and administrative agencies at various levels, including those at the grassroots, and provided the frontier

troops with facilities to carry out effective defence.

Passes: As military strongholds on the Great Wall, the passes were built on precipitous terrain on high mountains, in deep valleys or at key locations along a river or gulf. The basic purpose of each pass was to use a small force to resist a large number of invaders, while the structures themselves varied with the importance of the location and its topographical features. A simple pass would have only two walls, each with a gate. A complicated one would have a number of walls and fortified castles designed to protect one another, or could even look like a maze.

Platforms on the wall: Platforms, spaced from one another at a distance of 300 to 500 metres, were of three kinds:

One type was a relatively low platform with walls on the four sides, which were either crenelated or embrasured for the shooting of arrows.

A second type was the watchtower, generally two-storeyed and built of bricks. The lower floor could be supported by two, four or six arches, with the walls on the four sides embrasured for shooting purposes. The arched rooms provided lodging for the soldiers and were also used for the storage of food and fodder, arms and gunpowder. The upper and lower floors were linked by stairs or by a shaft, in which case the soldiers had to go up and down by a rope ladder. The upper floor had crenels and embrasures for watching and shooting at the enemy, and in some cases had a couple of rooms where the guards could stay or beat the watches with a clapper, light a signal torch or be on the lookout for enemy movements. A watchtow-

A watchtower may have three to six or even nine embrasures (windows through which arrows could be released). The picture shows a watchtower with nine embrasures, of which seven are still visible, while the other two have collapsed.

A square battle platform.

A round battle platform.

er generally had two gates but also could have one or three, with the gates facing the walkway on top of the Great Wall so that the troops could move in and out.

The third type was the blockhouse. It could have a square or round shape. It was always built on precipitous terrain and well furnished with arms, ammunition and other supplies for military action.

Historical records show that 1,200 watchtowers and blockhouses

These holes in the wall were used for throwing rocks at the enemy trying to climb to the top of the wall.

The embrasured battlements were to be used in combination with a row of barrier walls against an invading force.

were built on the Great Wall between Shanhai Pass and Beijing. Each watchtower was generally garrisoned by 60 officers and men, with half the number guarding the tower and the other half deployed behind the battlements on the wall. Fifteen jars of gunpowder, each weighing 150 kilogrammes, were ready for use by the men of each watchtower —stored there was also plenty of arrows, iron staffs and rocks they could find for dropping on the enemy through openings in the battlements.

The wall platforms, watchtowers and blockhouses, suited for both defensive and offensive action, represented advances in defence technology, particularly in the Ming period.

The body of the wall: The composition of the wall can be seen in the well-preserved sections near Beijing and Tianjin and in Hebei Province. Generally, the wall rests on a foundation of stone slabs, has a solid, rammed mixture of lime, sand and crushed bricks in the middle, and is faced with evenly-sized bricks. On a plain or in a hilly region it averages eight metres in height and six metres in width. In the mountains it varies in size with the terrain, generally being 8 to 10 metres high and 2 to 4 metres wide—but narrowing down to only 42 centimetres in width at certain points. On top of the wall on the outside face are battlements, which are provided with lookout holes in the upper parts and embrasures in the lower parts. The walkway on top of the wall is lined with a ditch that is complete with a number of holes for the drainage of water. This served to minimize rain damage to the wall and enabled the guards to store water whenever they needed to. In some cases several walls were built

across the walkway on top of the wall. Shielding one-third of the width of the walkway, they were used to hold off invaders who had fought their way to the top of the wall. In a few cases the body of the wall is embrasured on the side facing the enemy and is called *zhanqiang* (battle wall).

Beacon towers: They were also called "smoke towers" or "wolves' dung smoke towers" because various substances, including wolves' dung, were burnt to send up columns of smoke for military alarms. These towers were located at a distance of 5 or only 2.5 kilometres from each other and were usually built on elevations outside the Great Wall. Each tower had a storage of firewood, hay, sulphur and nitre for making fires. At the sign of an enemy invasion, military alarms would be signalled by letting off smoke during the day and lighting beacon fires at night, and the signals would be relayed from one tower to another over a long distance at good speed. During the Ming period the smoke and fire were accompanied by gunshots. It was stipulated that the coming of 100 enemy troops was to be indicated by one column of smoke plus one gunshot; of 500 enemy troops, by two columns of smoke plus two gunshots; of 3,000 or more, by three of each; and of 5,000 or more, by five of each. The speedy communication of frontline information enabled the garrison commander to make timely decisions.

The well-organized defences of the Great Wall were built by the arduous work of millions of workers. In addition to the frontier soldiers, the builders included conscripted labourers and convicts in exile. For example, when the Great Wall was first brought together under the direction of General Meng Tian over a period of 10 years during the Qin Dynasty, 300,000 troops were used. Later, a 450-kilometre section of the wall was built from Nankou, Beijing, to Datong, Shanxi, in 555 A.D. under the Northern Qi Dynasty, for which 1.8 million people were forced to join the ranks of the labourers.

Indigenous material was used for building almost all the sections of the wall. Earth, rocks and logs were used in the earlier periods. On a mountain the builders would quarry the rocks locally. On a plain they would gather earth and mix it with lime and mud before compressing the material between wooden boards. Most of the sections built in the Ming period were composed of bricks fired in nearby kilns.

The mountains, ravines, grasslands and deserts along the course charted out for the wall made construction a challenging task. In the Badaling section near Beijing, for instance, the wall had to rise and fall with the steep mountain slopes. Some of the stone slabs to be used there on the wall were two metres long and weighed one ton. It was no easy job to send the slabs and huge quantities of lime, bricks, etc. up to the mountain ridges; in fact, it would be a challenge today even with the modern means of transportation and construction now available. What the workers did was to open a number of trails winding up to the summits of the mountains and carry everything to the construction sites in baskets on their backs or shoulders. At times they would form a long line to pass the supplies hand to hand. Donkeys and goats were used as beasts of burden. The large stone slabs were inched along flat land on wooden rollers and moved uphill, step by step, by the use of crowbars—in either case a lot of people had to sweat.

Some sections of the wall show an ingenious use of the terrain. For example, mountain ridges were often paved with stone slabs on both sides to form a section of the wall, a method which saved building materials and achieved the purpose of controlling a strategic position. Or, using the steep bank of a river or the cliffs along a valley, the builders would make the wall high on the outside so it would be extremely difficult for the invaders to climb, but low on the inside so that the defenders could easily move about with their equipment and supplies.

With its many well-preserved sections, the Great Wall remains a symbol of the will power of the Chinese nation. The Chinese, who have always been reverent towards the dragon and who consider themselves to be descendants of the dragon, see the Great Wall as the symbol of a huge dragon active in the land of China. This conception can be best appreciated by ascending the wall itself.

The Great Wall at Simatai close to the Gubeikou Gateway in Miyun County, Beijing: It is complete with a watchtower, battlements and barrier walls.

A beacon tower for signalling military alarms.

The cliffs were used as part of the wall.

The Great Wall in Beijing, Tianjin and Hebei

The section of the Great Wall from Shanhai Pass to Mutianyu, almost 1,000 kilometres long, is the most beautiful part of the wall. It was governed by the Ji Garrison in the Ming period.

A STANDARD map of China usually shows the alignment of the Great Wall as built and renovated during the Ming Dynasty—which has largely been preserved as it was. The best preserved part of the Ming Great Wall lies in the municipalities of Beijing and Tianjin and in Hebei Province. This is the section of the wall which, running almost 1,000 kilometres from Shanhai Pass to Mutianyu, was administered by the Ji Garrison in the Ming period. Most parts of the wall here are built of stone slabs and faced with brick. The wall here—high and heavily fortified and having many towers and platforms—shows a variety of architectural styles. Passes and gateways have been built at all strategic points, numbering 32 between Shanhai Pass and Juyong Pass. Located on mountain ridges or in deep valleys, they are typified in these poetic lines:

The stacks of mountains tower beyond the clouds,
Cleaved in the middle by an awesome gateway,
Created by the will of Heaven.

The strategic positions of the defence barriers made it possible for relatively small numbers of garrison troops to cope with large forces of invaders. Among such barriers, the best-known ones in the section controlled by the Ji Garrison were Shanhai Pass, Xifengkou Gateway, Huangya Pass, Gubeikou Gateway and Juyong Pass.

Located to the northeast of Qinhuangdao in Hebei Province, Shanhai Pass leans against mountains and is skirted by the Bohai Gulf. It straddles the defile linking Northeast China with the Central Plains. Because of its strategic importance and the high-level of engineering, it has always been considered the No. 1 pass of the Great Wall and the key to the defence of two ancient capitals —Beijing in the east and Chang'an (Xi'an) in the west. First built in the year 583, the pass was renovated under various dynasties, being finally transformed into a formidable military stronghold during the Ming Dynasty. Its principal features are the Jiaoshan section of the Great Wall in the northwest and the main castle. There is also one supporting castle in the north and another in the south, as well as two semicircular protective walls in front of the main castle; and there are the towns of Weiyuan and Ninghai. Today the original main castle, the two supporting castles, and the two protective walls are still there. Other relics have been restored to their original forms, including the town of Ninghai, the Calm Sea Tower built on the wall of the town, and the Old Dragon's Head, a segment of the Great Wall extending into the sea. The "No. 1 pass" refers to the 25.7-metre-high east gate tower of the pass. The inscription on the lintel of the arched gate, reading "No. 1 Pass Under Heaven," was done in powerful strokes by Xiao Xian, a scholar with the highest imperial degree. The story goes that as he was planning the inscription, he was not happy with the way he did the 1.09-metre-long character *yi* (﹀), meaning "one." Then he watched how a waiter in a restaurant wiped the tables. Learning from the waiter's gestures, he finally did it well.

The Huangya Pass acquired its name from the yellow (*huang*) cliffs into which it was built. It was built across the Ju River in Jixian County in Tianjin. The pass and its round castle, Phoenix Tower, standing on the slopes north of the pass, have an imposing look. Unique along the whole length of the Great Wall is the Street of the Eight Diagrams lying below the pass, each composed of three whole or broken lines, which were used for divination in ancient China. An architectural wonder of the Ming period, the street was practically a labyrinth designed to confuse enemy invaders.

The section of the Great Wall near Beijing is well-preserved. The Yanshan Mountains lying northwest of Beijing, which rise like the shore of a sea gulf around the plain, seem to stretch their arms around the city. Likewise, the Great Wall, built along the ridges on these mountains, here curves in a semicircle. As the wall rises and falls with the various ridges, it is marked by different features. For instance, the Badaling section is known for its magnitude, the Mutianyu section for its precipitousness, and the Gubeikou Gateway for a combination of both.

Travelling past Changping County northwest of Beijing, one reaches an 18.5-kilometre-long valley called Guangou (Pass Gully), in which four barriers have been erected. The first one is Nankou (Southern Gateway); the second one, Juyong Pass; the third one, Shangguan (Upper Pass), which is now dilapidated; and the fourth one, the Badaling section of the Great Wall. Being north of Guangou, since ancient times Badaling has been referred to as the Northern Gateway, and the gate of the pass here has been compared to a lock of the gate. The wall averages 7.8 metres in height and has a width of 5.7 metres at the top and 6.5 metres at the base. The walkway on top of the wall is 4.5 metres wide, making it possible for five horses or ten soldiers to march abreast. A big, well-fortified tower is found along the wall every 300 to 500 metres. Looking at the wall from its base, one feels as though a huge dragon were flying skywards.

The Mutianyu section of the Great Wall is located northwest of the county town of Huairou. It winds its way a thousand metres to the top of a mountain before it dips downhill, forming a triangle like the horn of an ox. This is the well-known "Ox-horn Wall." Next to this is the precipitous terrain of Jiankou. The jagged cliffs here threaten to pierce the clouds and are a frightful sight to both men and beasts. The local people say that almost no eagles can fly over the peaks here.

Sections known as Jinshanling and Simatai guard the strategic Gubeikou Gateway in Miyun County. Arrayed to the east of the gateway, both were controlled by the Gubeikou garrison in the Ming period.

The Jinshanling section is virtually a museum of the architectural styles of Ming towers. As many as 67 towers are found within a distance of 10 kilometres. The towers are mostly two-storeyed and are square, round, oblate or, for those located at the corners, angular. An unusually big one is called "Storehouse Tower" because it has a storehouse on its southern terrace. It is protected by defence barriers, a wall in front, and an extra wall 60 metres downhill. Historical records show that the tower was used as the premises of a garrison headquarters.

Located to the east of the Jinshanling section, the Simatai section begins at the Simatai Reservoir. Here the wall travels along the ridges of high mountains and, at certain points, along cliffs formed by huge rocks, in which case the builders were able to create an impregnable wall by merely piling up a few layers of bricks. The most distinctive features of this section are perhaps the stone overpass and the stairs leading up to the Fairy's Tower. The stone overpass bridges the 900-metre-high peaks of the Kulong (Cavity) Mountain. It is 100 metres long and has a width varying from less than 40 centimetres to a little over 50 centimetres. It overlooks deep ravines on both sides. The overpass brings one to the "Heavenly Stairs," which lie along a mountain trail which is only wide enough for one person. The 30 or more stone stairs have a gradient of some 70 degrees and are each 60 to 70 centimetres wide, though only 30 centimetres are usable. A breeze would sway a person going up the stairs. The Fairy's Tower on top of the stairs is said to have been the habitat of a legendary fairy, who once even left an embroidered shoe there. East of the tower is the highest point in the Simatai section—the Tower for Viewing the Capital, from where on a clear autumn night people can sight the lights of Beijing. Though the Fairy's Tower and the Tower for Viewing the Capital are separated only by some 100 metres of the Great Wall, still no one has ever walked on this part of the wall—it is too thin and is sandwiched between cliffs. So after seeing the Fairy's Tower, visitors have to go downhill before climbing 1,000 metres to the Tower for Viewing the Capital. One question, however, remains unanswered to this day: how did the builders of the wall carry the bricks to such a great height?

The section of the Great Wall in Bijia Mountains, which lies between the Mentougou District of Beijing and Huailai County, Hebei Province, has so far drawn little public attention. The well-preserved wall, looking almost as gorgeous as a tiger's skin, and the wall's series of round towers combine to present an impressive sight.

The engineering quality and strategic value of the Great Wall sections in Beijing, Tianjin and Hebei are attributed to Beijing's importance as the capital of the Ming Dynasty. This part of the wall lies in a hilly land that lies between the northern fringes of the North China Plain and the encirclement of the Yanshan Mountains on the north, the Taihang Mountains on the west, and the Bohai Sea on the east. It is an area crucial to communication between the northern and southern parts of China and to the contact between the Central Plains and Northeast China, the Mongolian grasslands and Northwest China. The Ming court therefore had good reason to fortify the wall all the way from the coast to the Yanshan and Taihang mountains, building passes and strongholds and establishing garrisons at all the key points. But like all defence barriers, the wall had only a relative value. Towards the end of the Ming Dynasty, the peasant insurgents headed by Li Zicheng breached through the Juyong Pass and occupied Beijing, fighting with swords and spears and iron pellets fired from cannons. Upon this, the last emperor of Ming, Chongzhen, hung himself from a tree in today's Prospect Hill Park. Though the Ming Dynasty fell, the Ming Great Wall remains, standing as a silent witness to the past.

Map of the Great Wall in Beijing, Tianjin and Hebei

The Jiumenkou Gateway lies on the border between Liaoning and Hebei. There used to be a pass built across a river. Nine sluice gates were installed under the pass to regulate the flow of the river and hold off any invading enemy. The sluice gates rested on piers built of granite slabs, and the piers were linked by U-shaped iron loops. The local people refer to the pass as "a row of stone piers." The pass has suffered serious war damages, but retains its contours even today.

Sandaoguan used to be an important stronghold on the left of Shanhai Pass. It lies midway between the pass and Jiumenkou, being five kilometres from either location. High walls were built along both sides of the ravine shown in the picture, while three barriers were erected across the bottom of the ravine, with a stone gate serving as the only opening of the third barrier. The first and second barriers have both collapsed, and so has the stone gate on the third. But the ruins can still give people some idea of the ancient saying: "When one soldier holds a strategic pass, even ten thousand soldiers can hardly break in."

This is the Great Wall at Yiyuankou, the site of a gateway well known during the Ming Dynasty but which is hardly visible today.

This elevated platform, a few hundred metres from Jiumenkou, was used to relay military information sent from the beacon towers beyond Shanhai Pass to the national capital. It was the equivalent of the head office of a modern communications network.

The story of the young lady, Meng Jiangnü, bringing down the Great Wall by her tears is known to practically every Chinese. The story, which has circulated ever since the 7th century, says that she travelled a long distance from Shanxi to take winter clothes to her husband, a conscripted labourer working at Shanhai Pass. Learning that he had died from the backbreaking labour, she wailed for several days and nights, until the Great Wall collapsed along a stretch of 400 kilometres, revealing the bones of her husband among the rubble. At some unknown time, people built a temple for Meng Jiangnü on the Fenghuang Mountain seven kilometres east of Shanhai Pass. The picture shows her statue in the temple.

The Bianqiangzi beacon tower is located on high terrain five kilometres east of Shanhai Pass. Leaning against the Great Wall on the north and overlooking the Bohai Sea on the south, it is 8.5 metres high, including a square base which is 2 to 3 metres high and 50 metres in circumference.

Located to the northeast of Qinhuangdao, Shanhai Pass is protected by mountains and skirted by the sea coast. It straddles the passageway between Northeast China and North China, and has always been considered the "No. 1 Pass Along the Great Wall" in terms of both strategic importance and engineering quality. It was first built in 583 and renovated through the various dynasties until it acquired its present shape under the Ming Dynasty. It consists of the main castle, one supporting castle in the north and another in the south, two semicircular protective walls in front of the main castle, the town of Weiyuan, the town of Ninghai, plus the Jiaoshan section of the Great Wall in the northwest. Today most of these structures are still well kept, while some of the other relics have been restored, including the wall of Ninghai, the Calm Sea Tower built on the town wall and the Old Dragon's Head, a segment of the Great Wall extending into the sea. The picture shows the east gate of the pass, where the wall is 12 metres high and the tower 13.7 metres high. The two-storeyed tower has 68 embrasures or "arrow windows" on the north, south and east sides. The upturned eaves at the four corners are decorated with animal patterns. The inscription on the lintel of the gate, meaning "No. 1 Pass Under Heaven," is in the handwriting of Xiao Xian, an imperial scholar of the Ming Dynasty.   (Opposite)

Shanhai Pass

Weiyuan Hall

To Jaoshan section of the Great Wall

Gate of Far-Reaching Influence

Linlü Gatetower

East Gate

East protective walls

Gate of Blessings

Ramp passage for horses

Muying Gatetower

Main castle of Shanhai Pass

West protective walls

Gate Overlooking the Sea

Tower for the Pacification of Remote Areas

To Old Dragon's Head

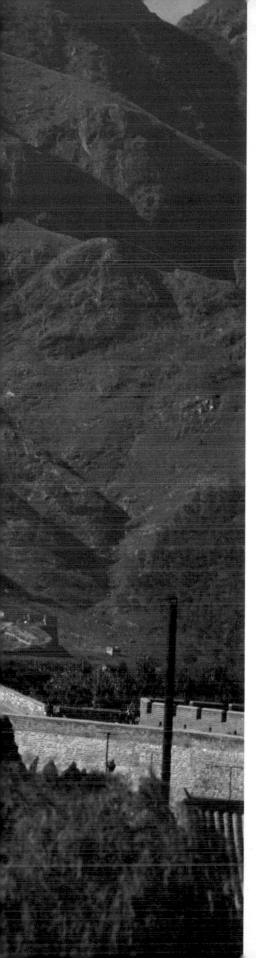

Tall and strongly built, the main castle of Shanhai Pass is contiguous to the Jiaoshan section of the Great Wall. (Top left)

Shanhai Pass
Built in the middle of the 12th century, the main castle of Shanhai Pass is 4,363.5 metres in circumference and used to have an east wall of 1,350 metres in length, a west wall of 1,290 metres, a north wall of 636 metres, and a south wall of 1,087.5 metres. All the four walls had towers on top and protective walls in front. What remains today, however, is only the east wall plus the east gate and the protective walls in front. (Opposite)

A tower on the southeast corner of Shanhai Pass is called Jingyuanlou (Tower for the Pacification of Remote Areas). It was built in 1587, destroyed by Japanese gunfire in 1933, and rebuilt in 1986 in the style of the Ming Dynasty. (Top right)

A cannon of the Ming Dynasty cast from iron which is on display at Shanhai Pass.

The town of Ninghai, five kilometres south of Shanhai Pass, is a rectangular structure surrounded by a wall measuring 500 metres in circumference and seven metres in height. The front part of the wall extending into the sea looks like a dragon sporting with the water and is called the Old Dragon's Head. A stone stele on the wall bears an inscription meaning "A Wall on the Sea Built by the Will of Heaven" in the calligraphy of Qi Jiguang (1528-1587), a famous general of the Ming Dynasty who once served as commander of the Ji Garrison. The Calm Sea Tower is located in the rear part of the town of Weihai and faces the sea. It was destroyed by the gunfire of the Allied Forces of Eight Nations which invaded China in 1900. It was rebuilt according to the original shape in 1986.

Left: The Calm Sea Tower.
Below: The Old Dragon's Head.

The Jiaoshan section of the Great Wall served as a commanding height for the defence of Shanhai Pass. Located 2.5 kilometres north of the main castle of the pass, it is 519 metres above sea level. The slopes are steep, with the result that some of the stairs leading to the top of the wall are 0.9 metres high. (Top right)

This watchtower, accessible only by a narrow staircase, rests on an elevated rock in the Jiaoshan section of the Great Wall.

Located in Qianxi County, Hebei Province, the Xifengkou Gateway was an important stronghold west of Shanhai Pass. The present name, which means "Peak of Happiness," has developed from an earlier one meaning "Site for a Happy Reunion." It is said that there was a young man who yearned to see his father, who had gone to build the Great Wall. He travelled a long distance and finally found his father working at this site. Overjoyed after a separation of several years, both father and son died on the spot. The gateway cuts through the Panjiakou Reservoir.

The Great Wall enters the water of the Panjiakou Reservoir from a ridge on its east bank.

The wall starts again on the west bank of the reservoir to continue its journey. (Opposite, bottom)

This round blockhouse rests on a hill 300 metres north of Huangya Pass. Called the Phoenix Tower, it has a diameter of 16.5 metres and a height of 23 metres. The two-storeyed structure has living space for the guards and storage space for supplies. The blockhouse was renovated in 1976 in the style of the Ming Dynasty. (Top left)

The main castle of Huangya Pass, built across the Ju River some 20 kilometres north of Ji County in the municipality of Tianjin, was vital for the defence of the city of Jizhou (now Ji County). It was renovated in 1976. (Top right)

Most of the military installations put up at Huangya Pass in the Ming period have collapsed because of weathering and war damages. This picture shows a water gate, restored only recently, built for the diversion of mountain torrents. (Opposite)

Qi Jiguang, a famous general of the Ming period, was appointed commander of the Ji Garrison in 1567. He held the office for 16 years, during which time he completely renovated the 800-kilometre section of the Great Wall under his jurisdiction. In particular, he designed watchtowers which provided sufficient accommodation for the guards. The picture shows a stone statue of the general in front of Huangya Pass.

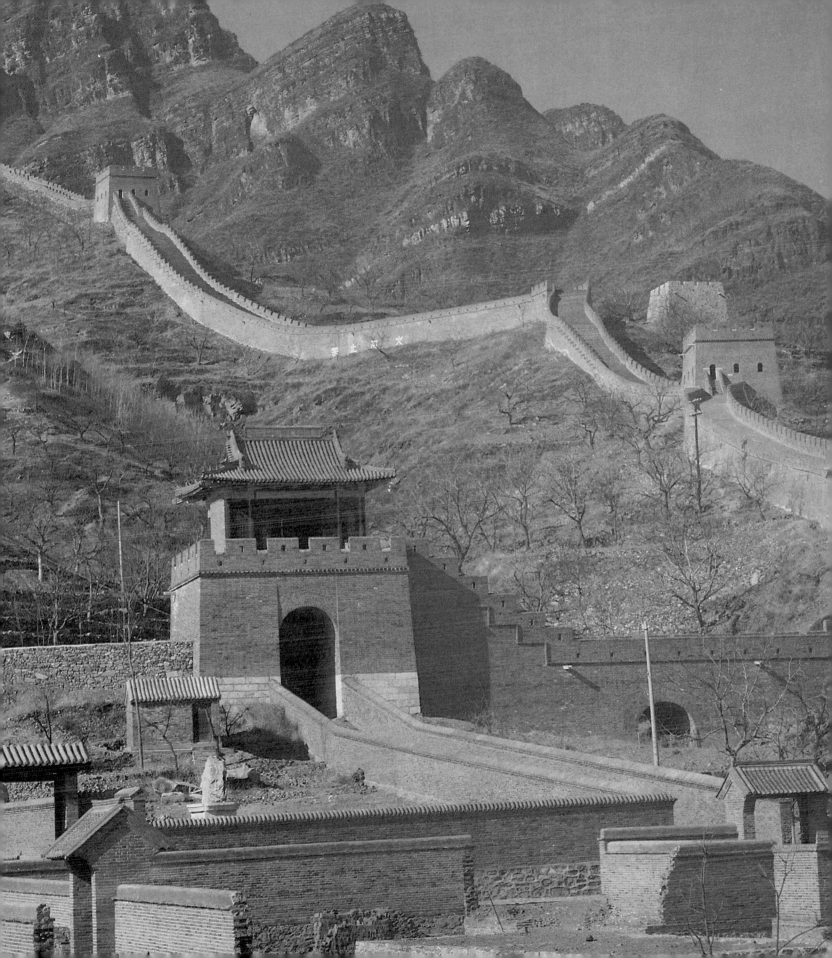

The Taipingzhai section of the Great Wall winds
its way around the peaks east of Huangya Pass. It
is unique structurally because brick and stone
materials alternate in the walls. The watchtowers
include both round and square ones. (Opposite)

The square watchtower in the distance, also in the
Taipingzhai section, is called Widows' Tower. It is
said to have been built by a labour force which
included the widows of 12 soldiers killed in action
in the Ming period.

The Tower of Avalokitesvara (Goddess of Mercy) is part of the Dule Temple in the city of Ji southwest of Huangya Pass. The city is over 2,000 years old. The tower, a 23-metre-high, two-storeyed structure, was built during the Tang Dynasty (618-907) and was rebuilt in 984. It is the oldest wooden tower existing in China today. Its peripheral columns rise gently towards the corners, where the eaves turn upwards. (Top left)

The statue of the Goddess of Mercy in the tower is 16 metres high and shows her 11 faces. It is one of the biggest clay sculptures in China and has stood the test of 28 earthquakes in the past 1,000 years.

There is a complex of imperial tombs of the Qing Dynasty (1644-1911) at Malanyu in Zunhua County, Hebei Province—they are referred to as Dongling (East Tombs). Covering an area of 2,500 square kilometres northeast of Ji County, it is the site of the tombs of five emperors, four empresses, one princess and five imperial concubines. The picture shows the tombs of Empress Dowager Ci'an and Empress Dowager Cixi. The coffin chamber and sacrificial hall of Cixi, the most powerful person in the last period of the Qing Dynasty, are unusually extravagant. Another complex of imperial tombs of the Qing Dynasty is located in Yi County, Hebei Province, to the southwest of Beijing and is referred to as Xiling (West Tombs). (Bottom left)

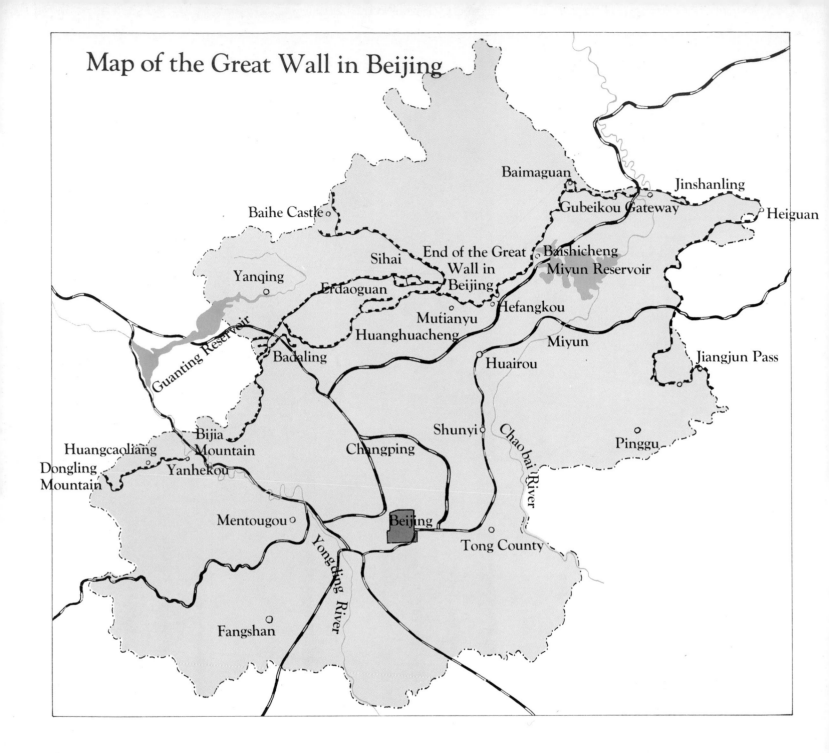

Map of the Great Wall in Beijing

Baimaguan

Jinshanling

Baihe Castle

Gubeikou Gateway

Heiguan

End of the Great
Wall in
Beijing

Baishicheng

Sihai

Miyun Reservoir

Yanqing

Erdaoguan

Hefangkou

Mutianyu

Miyun

Huanghuacheng

Jiangjun Pass

Badaling

Huairou

Bijia
Mountain

Shunyi

Pinggu

Huangcaoliang

Chungping

Dongling
Mountain

Yanhekou

Guanting Reservoir

Chaobai River

Mentougou

Beijing

Tong County

Yongding River

Fangshan

Map of the Great Wall in Beijing
The section of the Great Wall lying within the
municipality of Beijing extends over the northern
hilly areas in a semicircular shape. It has a length
of 629 kilometres, of which 123 kilometres are in
good shape and the rest in ruins or barely
traceable. Of the 827 platforms on the wall, only
391 are well-preserved.

The Storehouse Tower is a conspicuous structure along the Jinshanling section of the Great Wall. It is a large, two-storeyed watchtower protected by a wall in front and an extra wall 60 metres downhill. A storehouse is found on the southern terrace, which gave the tower its name.

Tourist Map of Gubeikou
There used to be three passageways between Northeast China and the Mongolian Highlands on the one side and Beijing and the Central Plains on the other. These were Shanhai Pass, Juyong Pass and the Gubeikou Gateway, the latter lying between the two passes and being located in today's Miyun County northeast of the city of Beijing. Gubeikou was the site of incessant warfare and was heavily guarded by the armies of various dynasties from the 7th to the 13th centuries. In particular, the Ming Dynasty (founded in the 14th century) added many defence installations and increased the strength of the garrison. By now, however, the main castle no longer exists, while much of the wall has collapsed. Only the Jinshanling and Simatai sections six kilometres to the east remain in fairly good shape. The great variety of defence structures here are good examples for studying the architecture of the Great Wall.

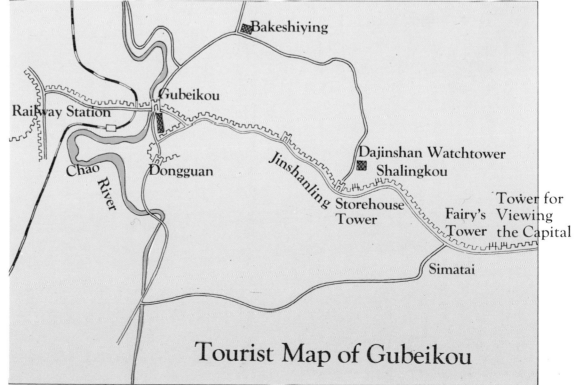

Tourist Map of Gubeikou

47

A long-distance view of the Storehouse Tower.

A close-up of the Storehouse Tower. Unusually big
and well fortified, it contained the command
headquarters. (Top right)

A full view of the Jinshanling section, which has a concentration of watchtowers spaced at 100 metres from each other—sometimes being spaced only 50 to 60 metres on difficult terrain. The watchtowers are two-storeyed and come in a variety of shapes.

Though decrepit, the Jinshanling section had a dignified look even before its renovation.

The Jinshanling section as viewed from the Simatai Reservoir to its east. (Opposite)

Jinshanling at dawn.

The Simatai section of the wall was built along the ridges east of the Simatai Reservoir. The 1,000-metre section rises and falls with the slopes. This picture shows a part of it.

The stone overpass at Simatai bridges the 900-metre-high peaks in the Kulong (Cavity) Mountain. Forming part of the Great Wall, the overpass is 100 metres long and varies from less than 40 centimetres to just over 50 centimetres in width. (Top opposite)

A row of barrier walls were built in front of a watchtower to hold off invaders.

More than 30 barrier walls were built uphill along a slope with a gradient of 70 degrees with a walkway mere 30 centimetres wide on the right side. The ingenious device, suited to both defence and attack, is called a "heavenly staircase."

The Tower for Viewing the Capital, almost 1,000 metres above sea level, is the highest point of the Simatai section. Here one can see the lights in Beijing on a clear autumn night. (Top right)

The ridge west of the Tower for Viewing the Capital looks like the scaled back of a fish. It is lined with a part of the Great Wall which is too narrow for people to walk on. The Fairy's Tower rests on a hill. (Bottom right)

The barrier walls are linked to the battlements for effective defence. (Opposite)

The main castle of Mutianyu is unique in that it has three watchtowers standing in a row.

Tourist Map of Mutianyu
The Mutianyu section of the Great Wall lies in Huairou County 70 kilometres northeast of the urban districts of Beijing. The main castle was built in 1404. The wall is crenelated on both sides, while the towers stand along the outer sides of the cliffs. In particular, the wall at Jiankou west of Mutianyu travels along precipitous peaks and shows how the builders utilized strategic terrain.

There are 22 watchtowers along a distance of 2,250 metres in the section open to tourists at Mutianyu. Walking in a northwest direction, one sees a lush growth of grass and trees, including ancient pines. More than 80 percent of the environment is covered by vegetation.

Tourist Map of Mutianyu

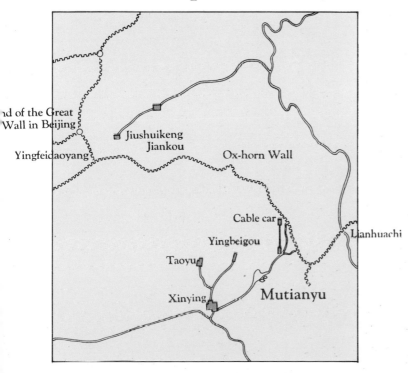

nd of the Great
Wall in Beijing

Yingfeidaoyang

Jiushuikeng
Jiankou

Ox-horn Wall

Cable car

Yingbeigou

Lianhuachi

Taoyu

Xinying

Mutianyu

Mutianyu
under snow.

The people of Beijing like to go to the Great Wall at Mutianyu in March or April every year, when the fields are ablaze with peach blossoms.

The Mutianyu section of the Great Wall rises to an 1,000-metre-high peak in the north and then goes downhill, forming, on the back of the hill, a triangle which looks like the horn of an ox. The "Ox-horn Wall" leads to a segment of the wall called Jiankou. (Opposite)

Jiankou, part of the Mutianyu section, runs 3,000 metres from east to west. It remains in fairly good shape. This segment of the wall surprises people with its sharp peaks and sudden drops that follow the precipitous slopes. One wonders how the builders managed to construct the wall on such difficult terrain.

A full view of the wall at Jiankou.

The west end of Jiankou in mid-autumn. The wall, set against a desolate background, has a dignified and ancient aura.

71

The jagged rocks look parti-coloured after a snow.

A pair of "sister pine trees" stand on a hill 800 metres above sea level. They are believed to be more than 300 years old.

Here the Great Wall rises to the peaks in the distance, which are said to have "turned eagles upside down." In other words, no eagle can fly over these peaks. Experts still do not agree on the way builders of the wall carried bricks and stones up to the peaks. (Opposite)

A few stone statues stand on a terrace along the highway 400 to 500 metres from the pass of Badaling. There used to be a temple here, housing a number of Buddhist stone statues. The temple has long since disappeared. Now the statues, originally erected to frighten away ghosts like those of the King of the Infernal World and the Guardian of Earth, are left in the open air.

Starting from Beijing and passing through Qinghe, Shahe and Changping, one arrives at Nankou in the north and then enters a valley called Guangou (Pass Valley). Four passes were built across the valley here in thé Ming period. The first one was Nankou, followed by Juyong Pass, Shangguan and Badaling. Today Nankou is a small industrial town where the pass has disappeared altogether, while Shangguan is hardly traceable. The picture shows Juyong Pass, which means "Pass of Conscripted Labourers," a name attributed to the great numbers of slaves and convicts moved here by the First Emperor of Qin to build the Great Wall. Zhu Di, Emperor Chengzu of the Ming Dynasty, gave the name of "Lush Greenery at Juyong Pass" to the pines and cypresses covering the hills here and designated the site as one of the Eight Views of Yanjing. (Yanjing is one of the old names of Beijing.)

Tourist Map of Badaling

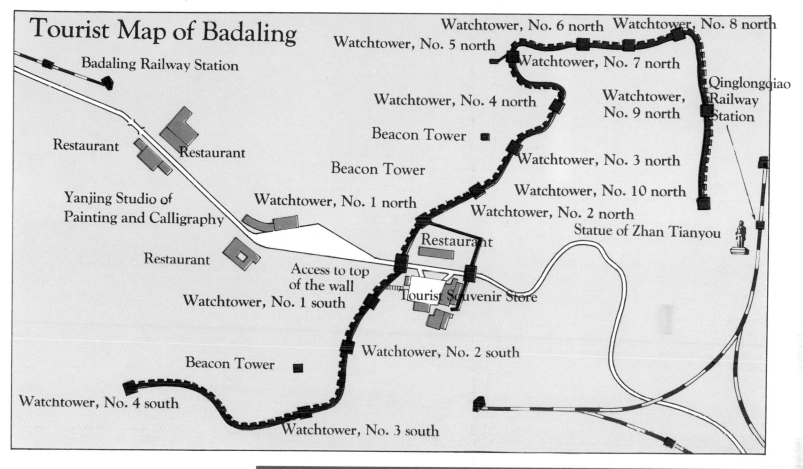

Badaling Railway Station

Watchtower, No. 6 north
Watchtower, No. 8 north
Watchtower, No. 5 north
Watchtower, No. 7 north
Qinglongqiao Railway Station
Restaurant
Restaurant
Watchtower, No. 4 north
Watchtower, No. 9 north
Beacon Tower
Yanjing Studio of Painting and Calligraphy
Watchtower, No. 1 north
Beacon Tower
Watchtower, No. 3 north
Watchtower, No. 10 north
Restaurant
Restaurant
Watchtower, No. 2 north
Statue of Zhan Tianyou
Access to top of the wall
Restaurant
Watchtower, No. 1 south
Tourist Souvenir Store
Watchtower, No. 2 south
Beacon Tower
Watchtower, No. 4 south
Watchtower, No. 3 south

Tourist Map of Badaling
One of the better examples of the Great Wall, the Badaling section slithers along the mountains and valleys 60 kilometres northwest of Beijing. Because of its strategic position, it has always been contested by opposing armies. The wall here was rebuilt to a greater height and strongly fortified during the Ming Dynasty in the 16th century as part of the effort to resist invasion by ethnic groups living in the north. People once compared the pass to a lock on the gateway to Beijing.

The walkway on top of the Badaling section is wide enough for five horses or 10 persons to travel abreast. The watchtowers are generally two-storeyed and over 10 metres high.

Badaling in Summer.

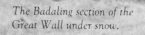
The Badaling section of the Great Wall under snow.

The northwest segment of the wall at Badaling.

A segment of the wall on the east side of Badaling which is not open to tourists. Though part of the wall has collapsed, people can still see how centuries ago builders used the rocks on the mountains as a natural part of the wall and chose precipitous terrain for the erection of forts. (Opposite)

Leaving Badaling, the Great Wall travels southwest to enter the Bijia Mountains lying in

Huailai County, Hebei Province, close to the Mentougou District of Beijing. The wall along the ridges of the mountain, built of rocks, remains in good shape; the watchtowers, either round or square, are built of bricks. The surface of the stone wall has fallen off or is covered with moss. These three pictures show scenes of the wall in the Bijia Mountains.

The wall running uphill in the Bijia Mountains at dusk. **(Opposite)**

The Gate to the Great Territory was built in 1368, the first year of the Ming Dynasty, as one of the passes along the Great Wall. A watchtower was added and the wall was made higher during the Qing Dynasty for better defence. The inscription on the lintel, meaning "Beautiful Mountains and Rivers," is in the calligraphy of Gao Weiyue,

governor of the Chahar region under the Qing Dynasty.

The Ming Great Wall in the Zhangjiakou area of Hebei Province extends over 500 kilometres, with part of it being well preserved. The picture shows the Dajingmen (Gate to the Great Territory) in the city of Zhangjiakou and the adjoining Great Wall.

Protected by the Great Wall, the city of Beijing was built over and again under different dynasties. The city's final shape was symmetrical, being laid out along a central axis running through the South-Facing Gate, Gate of Heavenly Peace and the Gate of Earthly Peace. The palace complex at the centre was flanked by neat streets and alleys. Imperial gardens and palaces for temporary stay by the royal family were added, some in the suburbs. The city has been enlarged and modernized since it became the capital of the People's Republic in 1949. **(Opposite)**

The Forbidden City, now called the Palace Museum, occupies an area of 720,000 square metres and has both large and small buildings consisting of 9,999 bays enclosed by 10-metre-high purple-red walls. Here are the palaces of the Ming and Qing dynasties, from which more than 20 emperors lived and administered state affairs.

Zhongnanhai (Central and South Lakes) and Beihai (North Lake) Park west of the Forbidden City and the Prospect Hill Park to its north were all imperial gardens in the Ming and Qing

periods. Now these parks, with their clever combinations of hills, groves and lakes, are scenic spots in Beijing's urban districts.

This picture shows the Hall of Prayer for Good Harvest in Beijing's Temple of Heaven. Located in the southern part of the city, the temple was the place where, at the beginning of each year, emperors of the Ming and Qing dynasties prayed for a good harvest. They also came here to pray for rain on the summer solstice and to offer sacrifices to Heaven on the winter solstice. The Hall of Prayer for Good Harvest was designed in a way to show reverence for Heaven and to pay respect to the gods. The circular hall and the square wall surrounding it correspond to the ancient hypothesis of a round heaven and a square earth. The building is covered with glazed deep-blue tiles. Each staircase has nine steps, symbolic of the nine layers of heaven described in ancient cosmology. On the night before the 15th day of the first lunar month, the emperor was required to bathe himself and abstain from meat and wine in order to prepare to come to the hall the next day to pray for a good year.

The Huanqiu (Circular Mound), another important structure in the Temple of Heaven, is a three-tiered circular marble platform. The circular piece of marble at the centre of the top tier fans out into concentric circles of slabs. On all three tiers the slabs of marble are laid out in multiples of nine, symbolic of the nine layers of heaven. The Circular Mound is enclosed by a blue-tiled double wall—the outer of which is square, the inner circular—and the gates on all four sides are decorated with patterns of floating clouds. Standing in the middle of the platform, one gets the feeling of being above the clouds. The Emperor of Heaven was believed to have his palaces above the "nine heavens," and the emperor in the temporal world, as the Son of Heaven, had to ascend the platform on the winter solstice every year to offer sacrifices to his father. (Opposite, bottom left)

The Summer Palace, 15 kilometres northwest of urban Beijing, boasts over 100 structures in a variety of classical styles. It was built under emperors of the Qing Dynasty over a period of more than 100 years, during which time enormous sums of money were spent to create the green hills and clear waters, pavilions and corridors in this imperial garden. The picture shows the Tower of Buddhist Incense on one of the hills and the Marble Boat on the Kunming Lake.

The Reed Gully Bridge, also known as the Marco Polo Bridge, was built in 1189. Being 265 metres long and eight metres wide, it is the oldest stone arch bridge in Beijing. The bridge straddles the Yongding River 15 kilometres southwest of the city. The balusters are decorated with 485 stone lions in a great variety of postures; some lions are clearly visible and others not so easy to detect. When Emperor Qianlong of the Qing Dynasty came to the site under the moon at daybreak, he gave it the name of "The Moon over Reed Gully Bridge at Dawn" and wrote the characters, which have been inscribed on a stone stele.

In addition to their palaces in Beijing, the Qing emperors also had a palace complex in today's city of Chengde, Hebei Province, by the side of the Great Wall. It is called the Mountain Resort for Avoiding Summer Heat. Built over a period of 89 years beginning in 1703, the resort is the epitome of all the scenic spots of China, as can be seen from its towers and pavilions, streams and lakes. The wall of the resort, 10 kilometres long, is called a miniature Great Wall. (Top opposite)

The Hall of Refreshing Mist and Waves in the palace complex in Chengde served as the bedroom for Qing emperors.

The Temple of the Potaraka Doctrine, located just outside the imperial resort in Chengde, was the place where Qing emperors received princes and noblemen of China's ethnic minorities. The temple is a scaled-down version of the Potala Palace in Lhasa, Tibet. (Bottom)

The Purple Great Wall in Shanxi

Sections of the Great Wall lying in the northern part of Shanxi Province are called "the Purple Great Wall" because the wall as well as the beacon towers are built of a mixture of red and yellow earth, which gives them a purple colour.

SECTIONS of the Great Wall in Shanxi Province acquired the name of "Purple Great Wall" from the colour of the wall, the beacon towers and the battle platforms in the region—the locality's yellow earth, mixed with red earth, made these structures look purplish.

Running northwest from Beijing, the wall cuts through the Zhangjiakou area in Hebei Province, turns southwest, passes Zhenkoutai in Tianzhen County, Shanxi Province, and enters the loess plateau in northern Shanxi. Bordering on the Great Desert in Mongolia while shielding the Central Plains, including the Beijing area, Shanxi was naturally a region where the Great Wall had to be built and rebuilt through the dynasties. Walls with a total length of 3,500 kilometres were constructed under various regimes. The biggest effort was contributed by the Ming government, which established the Datong Garrison and the Taiyuan Garrison. Xu Da, the famous general who contributed to the founding of the Ming Dynasty, was once commander of the Datong Garrison. The Mings also considered the region strategic enough to build both an Outer Great Wall and an Inner Great Wall in Shanxi. The outer wall, which was extended from the wall at the Xuanfu Garrison in northern Hebei, goes through Tianzhen, Yanggao and Datong and travels past Zuoyun, Youyu and Pinglu before it reaches Pian Pass, having covered a distance of 540 kilometres. The inner wall was extended from the wall at the Zhenbao Garrison in central Hebei. Going south from the Zhenbao Garrison, it crosses the Taihang Mountains, winds its way around the Hengshan Mountains, advances to Yan-

men Pass, bypasses Ningwu, and finally joins the outer wall at Baiyangling in Pianguan County, exceeding a total of 700 kilometres in length.

Six passes established along the Inner Great Wall are historically famous. They are Juyong, Zijing and Daoma passes in Hebei, called the "three inner passes," and Yanmen, Ningwu and Pian passes in Shanxi, called the "three outer passes." All six served as important bastions for the defence of Beijing.

Yanmen Pass crouches halfway up the Yanmen Mountain northwest of Dai County. "Yan" means "wild goose" and "men" means "gate." So the name probably comes from the wild geese which used to fly through the gate of the pass. Among the more than 40 passes and gateways built along the Great Wall in Shanxi, Yanmen stands out as the strongest and the best-looking one. Leaning against awesome cliffs and being the only access to the mountain trails, it rests on unconquerable terrain, historically contested by China's strategists. This was the very place where the generals of the Yang family, known to almost every Chinese child, fought heated battles with the Liao (Khitan) army during the Northern Song Dynasty.

Ningwu Pass is located between Yanmen Pass on the east and Pian Pass on the west. The garrison here could send reinforcements to the two other passes whenever necessary for the defence of the Central Plains.

Lying in Pianguan County, Pian Pass faces the Mongolian grasslands in the north and the Pianguan River, a tributary of the Yellow River, in the west. It is favourably located for both defensive and offensive action. Frontier commanders considered it a

key stronghold on the first line of defences. During the 14th century the Ming authorities had four supplementary walls built here, three north of the pass and one to its south, which altogether were fortified with over 200 beacon towers and watchtowers to guard against any invasion by the nomadic peoples from the Great Desert in the north.

Speaking of the passes of the Great Wall in Shanxi, one should not forget to mention Niangzi (Women's) Pass. Located to the northeast of Pingding County, it is a key passage between Hebei and Shanxi. The present pass was built in the 16th century, but the old one existed as early as the early 7th century. On the orders of Li Yuan, the first emperor of the Tang Dynasty, his daughter, Princess Pingyang, assumed command at the pass with a contingent of women soldiers. This was quite an innovation in feudal times, when male authority reigned supreme and women were considered inferior to men.

Historical relics dating to various periods can be seen on both sides of the Great Wall in Shanxi. Among them are the complex of Buddhist temples in the Wutai Mountains, the Xuankong Temple—which still looks gorgeous one thousand years after its construction—in the Hengshan Mountains, and the Yungang grottoes near Datong. Most of the more than 51,000 Buddhist statues carved on the rock walls of Yungang date to the 5th century. Varying from a few centimetres to 17 metres in height, they are among the best of Chinese stone sculptures.

Desheng Castle
Yongjia Castle
Hongci Castle
Tianzhen
Shahukou (West Outlet)
Yanggao
Yungang
Youyu
Datong
Zuoyun
Hengshan Mountains
Pian Pass
Ying County
Pinglu
Pingxing Pass
Suo County
Wutai Mountains
Yanmen Pass
Ningwu
Dai County
Meng County
Taiyuan
Yangquan
Niangzi Pass
Heshun

Map of the Great Wall in Shanxi

Niangzi (Women's) Pass, originally called Weize (Reed Pond) Pass, straddles a key route between Hebei and Shanxi. It is surrounded by a maze of hills and valleys. The pass acquired its name because women soldiers were garrisoned in it under the commandership of Princess Pingyang, daughter of Li Yuan, the first emperor of the Tang Dynasty.

Located on the Yanmen Mountain northwest of Dai County, Shanxi, Yanmen Pass is one of the three outer passes along the Inner Great Wall. The pass is located on the summit of a hill accessible only by an ancient trail which winds its way up between cliffs. Built during the Tang Dynasty (618-907) and rebuilt under the Ming (1368-1644), it was well-known for its strategic importance. The castle measured one kilometre in circumference, the brick-and-stone wall rising six metres. There used to be a gate on the east, the west and the north. Today, however, people can only see a pair of stone lions, a couple of flag posts and a few stone steles apart from the remains of the arched gates.

These are the statues of General Yang Ye (?-986) and his wife, which stand in the ancestral temple of the Yang family in Dai County. The general became famous for his resounding victory over the Liao army, which was pushing into Yanmen in the early period of the Northern Song Dynasty (960-1127). He later was wounded in battle, was taken prisoner and thereafter died through fasting. His patriotic cause was carried on by his descendants, who won a series of victories in the Yanmen area. The story of the generals of the Yang family is known to practically every Chinese, old and young. (Top left)

Dai County was part of Yanmen Prefecture in early times. The building shown in the picture, found in present-day Dai County, is called "Tower for the Pacification of the Borders." It was built during the Ming Dynasty. The plaque hanging on the tower reads: "The Voice (of the Emperor) Reaches the Four Corners (of the Land)." Also found there are other plaques which praise the beauty of the tower or the might of the imperial army, reminding one of the many battles fought around the pass through the centuries.

While the Great Wall in Shanxi is generally built of rammed earth, the section at Yanmen Pass is a brick-and-stone structure, an indication of its military importance.

With its many beacon towers and watchtowers, the Baicaokou section of the Great Wall in Dai County is a well-preserved part of the wall in Shanxi. (Opposite)

Ningwu Pass is the centrally-located pass of the three outer passes along the Inner Great Wall. If the line along the three passes is compared to a shoulder pole, Ningwu Pass may be considered the fulcrum of the pole, supporting Yanmen Pass on the east and Pian Pass on the west.

The Great Wall at Pian Pass is where the Inner and Outer Great Walls rejoin. Four supplementary walls and over 200 beacon towers and watchtowers were built at Pian Pass under the Ming Dynasty to fortify the defences here. Today the continuous line of the purple wall is still visible, although most of the other structures are in ruins or have disappeared.

Pian Pass overlooks a tributary of the Yellow River on its west. Here the waters from the Yellow River meet the Great Wall before they turn west. The local people call the place the "Old Bull's Bend."

Built of rammed yellow earth, the part of the Inner Great Wall lying in Shuo County has stood the test of 600 years of wind and rain and still looks good.

While the Great Wall in Pinglu County is built of earth, the watchtower is a brick structure.

In the Ming period the entire Great Wall belt was divided into 11 garrison zones, including two in Shanxi -- the Datong Garrison and the Taiyuan Garrison. The Datong Garrison was responsible for the defence of the Outer Great Wall, which was supplemented by 827 beacon-and-smoke towers and 72 castles and was guarded by a force equivalent to one twelfth of the total strength of the nation's army. The picture shows the ruins of one of the castles. The wall no longer exists, but some of the beacon-and-smoke towers are still there. (Right)

One of the castles along the Great Wall stands atop the Yungang Grottoes. (Bottom opposite)

Fifty kilometres from the Great Wall, the Wutai Mountain is one of the four sacred mountains of Chinese Buddhism, the other three being Putuo in Zhejiang, Jiuhua in Anhui and Emei in Sichuan. The temples in the Wutai Mountain are devoted to the worship of Manjusri, the Bodhisattva of Wisdom. Buddhist structures appeared among the hills as early as the 1st century, a large complex being formed by the 17th century. In particular, the wooden structures dating from the Tang Dynasty are regarded by historians of architecture as gems of traditional civil engineering.

Looking dignified and exquisite, the stone archway in front of the Dragon Spring Temple on Wutai Mountain is a masterpiece of stone carving.

Built for defence purposes, the section of the Great Wall in Ying County now shelters the crop fields from windstorms. (Bottom)

Dating to 1056, this wooden pagoda in Ying County rises 67.13 metres high and has a diametre of 30 metres on the ground floor. It is the tallest extant Buddhist pagoda of wood in the style of a storeyed tower. (Bottom right)

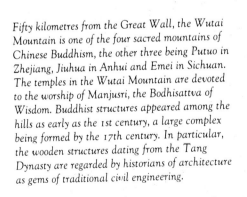

Extending over 10 kilometres from east to west, the Yungang Grottoes contain 53 main caves and 5,100 statues of Buddha, a cultural legacy of the Northern Wei Dynasty (386-534). (Opposite)

Slithering over the loess plateau, the Outer Great Wall divides Shanxi Province from the Inner Mongolia Autonomous Region.

The West Outlet lies in Youyu County, Shanxi Province, and borders on Inner Mongolia. Fleeing from famine, peasants of both Shanxi and Shaanxi provinces used to leave by the West Outlet to seek a living beyond the Great Wall. (Right)

107

The Concentration of Ancient Walls in Inner Mongolia

Visitors to the Inner Mongolia Autonomous Region enjoy the sight of its beautiful grasslands. It is also an area where they can find the densest concentration of the oldest sections of the Great Wall, an indication of the frequency of warfare in this part of China in ancient times.

Map of the Great Wall in Inner Mongolia

Erenhot

Urad Rear Banner
Urad Middle Banner
Langshan Mountain
Guyang
Dengkou County
Baotou
Hohhot
Horinger
Liangcheng
Ejin Horo
Fengzhen

∩∩∩∩∩∩∩∩∩ Jurchen Great Wall

⌐⌐⌐⌐⌐⌐⌐⌐ Qin Great Wall

▬▬▬▬▬▬ Ming Great Wall

A PASSAGEWAY called Sha-hukou in Youyu County, northern Shanxi, borders on the Inner Mongolia Autonomous Region. The passageway, also called Xikou (West Outlet), was the site through which three Mongol tribes—the Tumd, Ordos and Urad—used to send tribute gifts to the court in Beijing. The West Outlet was not a well-known location along the Great Wall until the later period of the Ming Dynasty, when natural calamities and incessant wars forced large numbers of peasants in Shanxi and Shaanxi to leave their homelands and move through this outlet to seek a living beyond the Great Wall. A folk song dating to those days runs like this:

My husband is leaving by the West
    Outlet;
I can hardly stop him, though I want
    him to stay;
The tears in my eyes I can't hold
    back.

The folk song, sung first along the Great Wall and then in other parts of China, has made the West Outlet famous.

Inner Mongolia boasts a concentration of the oldest sections of the Great Wall, the total length being over 15,000 kilometres. In addition to the Ming wall, walls built in the Warring States period and under the Qin, Han and Jurchen dynasties can also be seen here.

From the top of the Daqing Mountain north of Hohhot, capital of the Inner Mongolia Autonomous Region, one can see an ancient wall slithering along the slopes of the mountains which cut through the region, the Yinshan. This is the Great Wall built by the state of Zhao in the Warring States period. To-

wards the end of the 4th cen[tury] B.C., King Wuling of the stat[e of] Zhao carried out military reform[s] [be]cause he realized that his infa[ntry] and war chariots were no m[atch] for the cavalry of the Xiongnu [(the Huns). He ordered his troop[s to] dress themselves like nomads [and] learn the art of horsemanship [and] archery. His cavalry, the first o[ne to] appear on the Central Plains, [ad]vanced northward and occupied [the] whole region south of the Yins[han] Mountains. Round about 300 [B.C.,] the state of Zhao built its Great W[all] along the ridges of these mounta[ins.] The section that remains to this [day] is built of compressed earth and [is] hardly two metres high. It is on[e of] the oldest relics of the Great Wa[ll.]

A well-preserved section of [the] Great Wall built under the [Qin] Dynasty has been found in Guy[ang] County south of Hohhot. More t[han] 2,000 years old, it covers 90 k[ilo]metres, averages four to five me[tres] in height, and is mostly built [of] rocks.

The Great Wall built under [the] Jurchen Dynasty dates to the 12t[h or] 13th century. It extends over 5,0[00] kilometres from Morin Dawa in [the] northeastern part of Inner Mongo[lia] to the Yinshan Mountains on [the] west. The Jurchen people had [a] unique way of building the wa[ll.] They began by digging a dit[ch,] which also served a military purpo[se,] using the earth thus excavated [to] build a wall and erecting cast[les] wherever necessary. Their defen[ce] system is historically known as [a] series of frontier castles along [a] boundary ditch."

The Ming Great Wall trave[ls] along the border between toda[y's] Inner Mongolia Autonomous R[e]gion and Shanxi Province, and

The Yinshan Mountains cut across Inner
Mongolia. Beginning in the Warring States period,
sections of the Great Wall were built along the
ridges of the mountains under various dynasties.
The picture shows the wall of the Qin Dynasty in
Guyang County. With a length of 90 kilometres
and a height of four to five metres, it is the
best-preserved section of the Qin Great Wall.

This mountain pass, Langshankou, in Urad Middle Banner, Inner Mongolia, has been considered a strategic location down through the centuries. (Top opposite)

The Yinshan Mountains have provided homes for nomadic peoples like the Huns and Tujue in northern China. These carvings on the rocks in the mountains are the relics of their culture.

This is the tomb of Wang Zhao Jun in the southern suburbs of the city of Hohhot. Her marriage of Huhanye, king of the Huns, in 33 B.C. ushered in over 60 years of peace between the Huns and the Han regime. (Top left)

The Great Wall of the Han Dynasty (206 B.C.-A.D. 220) along the Yinshan Mountains was largely a renovation of the wall of the Qin Dynasty, although a great number of passes and castles were added. The Jilu Castle at the mouth of the Hargen Mountains in Dengkou County was one of these castles. It was located on an important road linking the Han empire with the Great Desert. In 51 B.C. Huhanye, king of the Huns, passed through here on his way to the Han capital of Chang'an (now Xi'an) and on his return trip. He married Wang Zhao Jun, one of the ladies of the Han palace. The picture shows the ruins of the foundation of the Jilu Castle. (Top right)

The Han Great Wall in Urad Rear Banner, Inner Mongolia.

The 5,000-kilometre Great Wall of the Jurchen Dynasty (1115-1234) enters the Yinshan Mountains after passing through the grasslands. The Jurchens established a regime which, after its rise on the northeast grasslands in the 12th century, rivalled the Song Dynasty. To build the wall they first dug a ditch and then used the earth thus excavated.

The Ming Great Wall at the West Outlet, which borders on Horinger County in Inner Mongolia. This was the place through which the Tumd, Ordos and Urad tribes of Mongolia sent their tribute goods to the Qing court in Beijing.

This is the famous Dazhao Temple in Hohhot, constructed under Altan Khan of the Tumd tribe and his wife, Lady Jin. They built the city of Hohhot in 1581 with the assistance of the Ming government. (Top opposite)

The hall for the recital of Buddhist scriptures in the Dazhao Temple.

This statue of Lady Jin is a relic of the Ming Dynasty. As wife of Altan Khan, who headed the Tumd tribe, she worked for friendship with the Ming empire and promoted commercial and cultural contacts with the Han people. Largely through the efforts of the Mongol stateswoman, cordial relations existed between the Mongols and the Hans for many years.

The mausoleum of Genghis Khan 15 kilometres southeast of Altan Xiret in Horinger Banner.

Genghis Khan (1162-1227), famous statesman and military strategist in Chinese and world history, was elected "the Great Khan" at a conference of Mongol noblemen in 1206. His troops first attacked Zhongdu (Middle Capital, today's Beijing) of the Jurchen Dynasty in 1211, capturing it during a second attack in 1215. Beginning in 1219, Genghis Khan conducted a series of campaigns and expanded his empire to Central and West Asia.

There are over 3 million people of the Mongolian nationality in China, most of them living on the Mongolian grasslands. They are characteristically brave and straightforward, and are good at horsemanship and archery.

Wrestling.

A horse race.

Traces of the Wall of the Qin Dynasty in Northern Shaanxi

The Great Wall lying in Shaanxi Province was built during the Ming Dynasty, largely on the ruins of the Qin wall. The original Qin wall is hardly traceable, but some of its castles and towers are still there. Thus historians call this part of the wall "a Great Wall lined with castles of the Qin Dynasty." The picture shows a beacon tower of the Qin period standing on the cliffs in Shenmu County.

This is the Zhenbeitai (Pacify-the-North Tower) in Yulin, which was one of the 11 garrisons along the Great Wall in the Ming period. Five kilometres north of Yulin, the beacon tower was built in 1587 for the protection of the Hongshan Market Place —where the Mongol and Han people traded their goods. Being the biggest beacon tower along the Great Wall in the Ming period, the four-storeyed structure is 30 metres high and 130 metres in circumference and occupies on area of 5,050 square metres.

Yulin first became a military stronghold in the Han Dynasty. Through the centuries the Great Wall there has been rebuilt over and again. Today, however, people can see little more than the wall of the Ming period.

The Great Wall in Yulin extends over 200 kilometres and is lined with 210 beacon towers and battle platforms.   (Top right)

The Red Stone Gorge north of the county town of Yulin is a scenic spot beyond the Great Wall. With a stream running between jagged cliffs, the site has long been frequented by poets and writers. They would come here to drink wine and compose poems —often with the lines afterward being inscribed on the rocks. People can still see these inscriptions, which show how the poets felt about the Great Wall and which express good wishes for peace and friendship among China's different ethnic groups.

Jiaxian, a small county town in
northern Shaanxi, rests on the cliffs by
the side of the Yellow River. Because of
its terrain, it has always been easy to
defend the town and difficult to capture
it. It seems to enjoy the same advantages
even today.

A castle built in the Ming Dynasty in Mizhi, a county in northern Shaanxi, seems to still play its old role of guarding the caves in the mountain villages.

This is where Shaanxi, Inner Mongolia and Ningxia join each other—a strategic zone historically contested by ethnic groups in northern China. The winner was then poised to conquer the Central Plains. Tired of the incessant wars, the local people gave their towns names like Dingbian, Anbian and Jingbian, which essentially mean "pacification of the border" or "peace on the border." The picture shows the Great Wall in Jingbian.   (Top opposite)

The Great Wall in Anbian, looking as though it were guarding the wheat fields.

· The Great Wall in Dingbian has almost been swallowed by the desert.

The quiet front yard of a peasant's family —typical of life along the Great Wall in northern Shaanxi today.

Practically every city in northern China has been or still is surrounded by a wall. The picture shows the city wall of Xi'an, a metropolis rebuilt under the Ming Dynasty in the 14th century on the site of the old city—Chang'an, the capital of the Tang Dynasty.   (Top opposite)

Terra cotta figures in the mausoleum of the First Emperor of Qin, who employed a great workforce of almost a million to erect the Great Wall for its defence and established a big army for military expeditions.   (Bottom opposite)

The tomb of Huo Qubing (140-117 B.C.), a famous general of the Han Dynasty who died young, is located in Xingping County, west of Xi'an. Active during the reign of Emperor Wu, he conducted six campaigns against the Huns and opened the communication lines between the Gansu Corridor and the Western Regions (the latter being today's Xinjiang as well as Central and West Asia). In memory of the general's exploits, Emperor Wu had 14 stone sculptures erected in front of his tomb, of which the best-known one shows a horse treading on a Hun.

This is one of the fine horses carved on stone in front of the tomb of Li Shiming (599-649), Emperor Taizong of the Tang Dynasty. It is considered one of the best examples of Chinese stone carving.

The Great Wall Skirting the Ningxia Plain

The Great Wall in today's Ningxia Hui Autonomous Region runs a distance of 500 kilometres along the ridges of the Helan Mountains. Of the 37 passes and gateways in these mountains, the Sanguankou Gateway—lying in the middle and being the key link between the Alxa Plateau in Mongolia and the Ningxia Plain —had to be guarded most carefully. The picture shows the Ming Great Wall at the Sanguankou Gateway.

PASSING by the Mu Us Desert, the Great Wall continues its journey in a northwest direction to reach a region of oases with their adjoining fields and rows of trees. This is the Ningxia Plain, reputed to be like the areas south of the Yangtze River in greenery and fertility. It lies in the northern part of today's Ningxia Hui Autonomous Region. (The Hui is an ethnic group in China which follows the Islamic faith.)

Located between the Yellow River on the east and the Helan Mountains on the west, the Ningxia Plain was considered to be both a barrier protecting the Central Shaanxi Plain and also a lock on the gateway to the Gansu Corridor. Here the Yellow River has been utilized for irrigation since ancient times, and the fields are crisscrossed by ditches and canals. Rulers of successive dynasties called the area "a granary along the Great Wall." Because of the region's riches and strategic importance, local people have continuously maintained the wall here. The effort, which started in the Warring States period, culminated in the construction of 1,500 kilometres of the wall in all four directions during the Ming period. What is called the East Great Wall starts at Dingbian in Shaanxi and branches into two walls as it goes west, one passing through Yanchi in Ningxia, and the other passing north of Yanchi, meandering along the southwest border of the Mu Us Desert. The two walls run parallel, keeping a distance from each other of a few dozen to a hundred kilometres. They join into one again in the vicinity of Caijialiang, go westward to the Hengshan Castle, enter the Yinchuan Plain, and proceed north along the Yellow River. The North Great Wall, located in the northern part of the area irrigated by the Yellow River, also branches out into two walls. One starts from Hongguokou in the city of Shizuishan to reach the banks of the Yellow River on the east, while the other, located to the south begins at Dawukou and also goes east to arrive at the side of the river. The two walls run parallel from east to west between the Helan Mountains and the Yellow River, barring the passages from the Mongolian highlands to the Ningxia Plain. The West Great Wall runs from north to south across the Helan Mountains. Going through the Sanguankou gateway and Shengjing Pass, it leaps over the Yellow River in Zhongwei County to enter Gansu in the south. The wall was built in this way because the northern tip of the Ningxia Plain is sandwiched between the Mu Us Desert and the Tengger Desert and the rulers of Ming were afraid that the Mongols would seize the tip by a pincer movement, taking the whole plain and threaten central Shaanxi. In addition to the Great Wall mentioned above and the natural barriers formed by the Helan Mountains and the Yellow River, the Guyuan Garrison was established and walls and passes were built in southern Ningxia as a second line of defence, called (not to be confused with the wall of the Shanxi Garrison) the "Inner Great Wall."

Quite a few sections of the Great Wall in Ningxia remain in good shape, though they have been weathered by the storms of several centuries. Any peak in the Helan Mountains would offer a clear view of these walls, reminding one of the mountains dotted with castles under white clouds in a sunny sky as described in ancient poetry. The city wall of Guyuan is in almost as good shape as the former city wall of Beijing. The Inner Great Wall in Guyuan, which lies in ruins, can still enable one to visualize how it once protected the Silk Road. The walls in Ningxia are mostly built of compressed yellow earth. The local people, including Huis and Hans, hardened it between wooden boards, layer after layer, before joining up the segments. The project cost much labour and even some lives, but it did help bring people peace and tranquility in some historical periods.

Map of the Great Wall in Ningxia

Hongguokou

Shizuishan

Shizuishan City

Taole

Helan Mountains

Yinchuan

Touguan

Lingwu

Caijialiang

Qingtong Gorge

Yanchi

Yellow River

Zhongwei

Tongxin

Guyuan

This is a beacon tower—built along the Ming Great Wall in Tongxin County—which served as an outpost for the important stronghold at Guyuan. If Tongxin were lost, it would be hard to defend Guyuan and the Central Plains would be exposed to the invading army. This was why the wall—a major undertaking—was built in Tongxin and its neighbourhood during the Ming Dynasty from 1502-1537.

Coming from Dingbian in Shaanxi, the Great Wall enters Yanchi County, Ningxia. There it becomes part of the Eastern Great Wall. The Ming authorities built a wall in Yanchi and supplemented it with another five kilometres to the south. The picture shows a section of the latter, which averages six to eight metres in height and remains in fairly good shape.

This is the first wall built by the Ming authorities in Yanchi. The wall, which extends into the distance, has worn down to less than two metres in height.

The Beichakou Gateway of the Qingtong Gorge is 50 kilometres south of the Sanguankou Gateway in the Helan Mountains. While the Great Wall in Northwest China is generally built of compressed yellow earth, the wall here is composed of rocks gathered from the Helan Mountains.

A unique grouping of 108 pagodas of the Yuan Dynasty (1271-1368) is located on the slopes to the west of the Qingtong Gorge Reservoir. Following the topography, the pagodas are arranged into an equilateral triangle by the odd numbers of one, three, five, seven, etc., from top to bottom. Buddhism believes that life suffers from 108 types of worries. To be free from all these worries, one must recite the Buddhist sutras 108 times, wear a

Buddhist necklace of 108 beads, and build 108 pagodas.

The Ming authorities established two garrisons in Ningxia: the Ningxia Garrison with headquarters in Yinchuan and the Guyuan Garrison with headquarters in Guyuan. The Great Wall built between the Helan Mountains and the Yellow River was the main defence barrier on the north side of the Ningxia Garrison. The picture shows the wall at the Hongguokou Gateway in Shizuishan. (Opposite, bottom left)

With the Yellow River on its west and Shanxi and Shaanxi on its east, Guyuan was a key passage between areas beyond the Great Wall and the

Central Plains. The Ming authorities placed here the headquarters of the military governor responsible for the defence of northern Shaanxi, Gansu and Ningxia. The picture shows the well-fortified city wall of Guyuan, which is tall and protected by a ditch. (Top opposite)

Guyuan was first named Yuanzhou. This is a renovated gate of the city wall. (Opposite, middle left)

The over 20 stone caves in Mt. Sumeru (near Guyuan) were hollowed out over a long period —from the 4th to the 13th centuries. They contain more than 100 statues of Buddha and of Bodhisattvas. (Opposite, bottom right)

The Zhenbeibao (Pacify-the-North Castle), 30 kilometres northwest of the city of Yinchuan, was built in 1500. According to historical records, its construction strengthened frontier defences to such an extent that the local people could "chop wood and graze the animals in peace." (Left)

Beginning in the Yuan Dynasty, large numbers of Moslems settled in Ningxia. There are more than 2,000 mosques in Ningxia today. This is the Nanguan Mosque in Yinchuan. (Bottom)

Yinchuan was the seat of the headquarters of the Ningxia Garrison in the Ming period. Many centuries-old structures are preserved in the city. Built at an unknown date, the Haibao Pagoda in the northern part of the city distinguishes itself from pagodas in other parts of China by its bright colours and powerful clear-cut lines.

The tombs of eight emperors of the Western Xia Dynasty (1038-1227), plus more than 70 tombs of those who were buried with them after immolation, are located in the east range of the Helan Mountains. The site occupies an area of four kilometres from east to west and 10 kilometres from north to south. The Western Xia empire, established by one of China's ethnic minorities,

controlled much of Northwest China, including Ningxia, until it was vanquished by the Mongols. (Top right)

On festive occasions Moslem families in China prepare sanzi, a ring- or coral-shaped cake. It is made of a mixture of sticky rice and flour seasoned with salt and fried in deep oil. A poet wrote about the making of the cake: "The jade-coloured flour is twisted and rolled by the nimble fingers of a lady; coming out of green oil, it looks delicious with a dark yellow colour."

The Ningxia plain owes its fertility to irrigation with water from the Yellow River. This squeaky waterwheel, essentially the same as those used in ancient times, continues to lift water from the river to the fields. (Bottom right)

Jiayu Pass
in the
Gansu
Corridor

GANSU Corridor in Northwest China borders on Shaanxi on the east and Xinjiang on the west. In ancient times it was an important link between the Central Plains and the Western Regions, a broad term which covered Xinjiang, Central and West Asia, and sometimes even India, Eastern Europe and North Africa. The caravans travelling through Gansu carried China's silks, porcelain and tea to the Western Regions, and brought back glassware and spices. This was the famous ancient Silk Road.

Crossing the Yellow River in Lanzhou, capital of Gansu, and climbing over the peak of Wushaoling northwest of Lanzhou, one comes to a narrow strip of land lying in an east-west direction. Butting up against the Longshou Mountains and Heli Mountains in the north and facing the Qilian Mountains and the Yingzui Mountain in the south, it is composed of one oasis after another in the shape of a corridor over 1,000 kilometres in length and from a few dozen to several hundred kilometres in width. Known as the Hexi or Gansu Corridor, the area was one of strategic importance to communications and military operations. The Great Wall was built over and again along the corridor through more than 2,000 years, during which time a total of some 8,000 kilometres of walls, plus a great number of passes and castles, were erected under various dynasties. King Zhao of the state of Qin, for example, built a wall in central Gansu in the Warring States period. The first continuous Great Wall, built by the First Emperor of Qin after he conquered the whole country in 221 B.C., had its western end at Lintao in Min County of present-day Gansu, and its eastern end in eastern Liaoning, 5,000 kilometres away. In the second century B.C. Emperor Wu of the Western Han established his authority over the Gansu Corridor in order to guarantee his communications with the Western Regions and defend against invasion by the Huns. To this end, a section of the Great Wall was built from the banks of the Yellow River in Lanzhou and extended over mountains and deserts until it reached Lop Nor in Xinjiang. The Han court established four prefectures west of the Yellow River —Wuwei, Zhangye, Jiuquan and Dunhuang—and placed strong garrisons there to protect the corridor. The phalanxes of bronze horses and chariots unearthed in Wuwei provide evidence to the rule of the Han Dynasty—one is a bronze galloping horse placing its right hind on a flying swallow. The name "Jiuquan," which means "wine spring," comes from a story about General Huo Qubing, to whom Emperor Wu sent a jar of palace wine to commend his army for having opened up the Gansu Corridor. Since the wine was too little for his soldiers, the general poured it into a spring so everybody could share some by drinking the water.

The Ming Great Wall branches north and south after it enters Gansu. The outer wall in the north starts from the west banks of the Yellow River and passes through Jingtai to reach Wuwei. The inner wall in the south, coming from Guyuan in Ningxia, passes by Jingyuan and Lanzhou, proceeds along the Zhuanglang River and crosses the peak of Wushaoling to join the outer wall at Tumen in Gulang County. Being the east gateway to the Gansu Corridor, Lanzhou was a hub of the Silk Road protected by the Fenghuang Mountain in the north and by the Gaolan Mountain in the south, while the Yellow River cuts through the city horizontally. Originally named Jincheng, the city was first built in the Sui Dynasty and rebuilt in later periods. In the Ming Dynasty the city was expanded, well fortified and heavily guarded with a wall of 1.5 kilometres in circumference, 17 metres high and 13 metres wide, enclosed by a 15-metre-deep moat on the east, west and south.

Seen outside Lanzhou is a section of the Han Great Wall running parallel to the Ming Inner Great Wall, both of which join the Ming Outer Great Wall in Gulang County.

Leaving Wuwei, the Ming Great Wall turns north along the east banks of the Shiyang River, passes by Minqin County, and comes back south along the west banks of the same river before it resumes its westward journey to reach Zhangye and then Jiayu Pass in the vicinity of Jiuquan. Located at the foot of the Jiayu Mountain some 20 kilometres from Jiuquan City, Jiayu Pass was the western end of the Ming Great Wall. The main castle of the pass has a floor space of 35,500 square metres and is surrounded by an east wall of 154 metres, a west wall of 166 metres, and a north and south wall of 160 metres each. The arched gates on the east and west are called Gate of Enlightenment and Gate for Conciliation with the Remote Peoples. Each of the two gates has a protective wall in front. Additional protection for the main castle is provided by a brick wall 20 metres to its west. A ditch two metres from this brick wall had originally been dug. For the main castle, the protective walls and the ditch were combined with the

Map of the Great Wall in Gansu

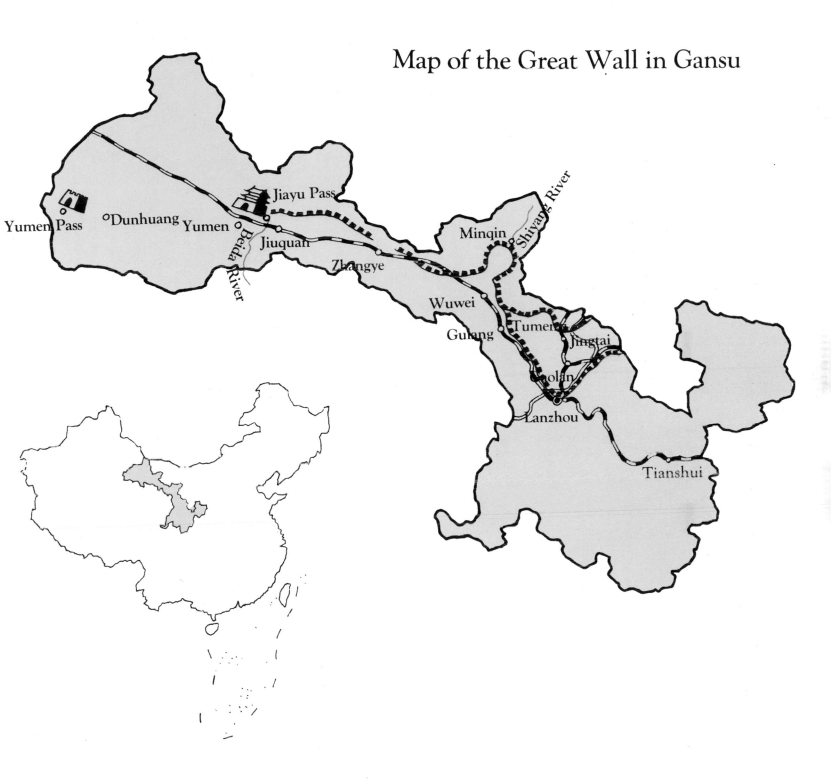

Yumen Pass

Dunhuang

Yumen

Jiayu Pass

Jiuquan

Beida River

Zhangye

Minqin

Shiyang River

Wuwei

Gulang

Tumen

Jingtai

olan

Lanzhou

Tianshui

Great Wall extending north and south and with the forts and beacon towers along the wall to form a complete defence system against almost any number of invaders.

Jiayu Pass is the western end of the sections of the Great Wall xtant. But the wall once extended further to the west—into the deserts, where its ruins can still be seen.

The Yellow River in Gansu.

Coming from Guyuan in Ningxia, the Inner Great Wall built in the Ming period enters Gansu and hits Lanzhou by way of Jingyuan. Lanzhou, capital of Gansu Province, was called Jincheng (City of Gold) in ancient times because of gold mining in the locality. Geographically it is at the centre of China's territory. It was always heavily guarded by the central dynasties as a strategic point along their northwest border and came to be known as "a city built of metal and protected by a moat of boiling water," a phrase which is still being used to describe any impregnable city. But today Lanzhou is a modern industrial city, where no traces of the Great Wall are to be seen. The picture shows the first iron bridge built across the Yellow River. Completed in 1907, the bridge is an important means of communication between east and west.

These are the ruins of the Great Wall at the peak of Wushaoling, a height which had to be crossed by both the Han and the Ming walls before reaching the Gansu Corridor. The picture shows the ruins of the Ming wall on the peak.

As part of the Qilian Mountains, the peak of Wushaoling lies in the Tianzhu Autonomous County of Tibetans. The Tibetan people have been living on the natural pastures in this locality for generations. At present they have basically settled in permanent homes, although they still pitch tents on the highlands in summer to graze their cattle and sheep there.

Beginning in the year 121 B.C., Emperor Wu of the Western Han Dynasty established four prefectures in the Gansu Corridor—Wuwei, Zhangye, Jiuquan and Dunhuang. Wuwei, previously named Liangzhou, is located at the east end of the corridor. It was developed by General Huo Qubing after his conquest of the Gansu Corridor and became the capital of one feudal separatist regime after another in various periods of Chinese history. Zhangye, originally called Ganzhou, was the seat of the headquarters of the Gansu Garrison, the westernmost defence setup of the 11 garrisons along the Great Wall in the Ming period. During the Sui (581-618) and Tang (618-907) dynasties it was crowded with merchants and had whole streets of shops —becoming a centre of trade with the Western Regions, including countries of Central Asia. Jiuquan, which means "wine spring," acquired its name from an episode in the time of General Huo Qubing. To commend him for his victories over the Huns, Emperor Wu sent him a jar of wine. The general poured it into a spring so that all of his soldiers could have some. Located at the west end of the Gansu Corridor, Dunhuang was a key prefecture, having jurisdiction over six counties and two passes along the Great Wall, Yang Pass and Yumen Pass. It has become world-famous for the Mogao Grottoes, 25 kilometres to its southeast. The grottoes were hollowed out from the 4th century onward, and people can see today 492 stone caves with 2,450 statues and 45,000 square metres of wall paintings.

Upper left: Bronze chariots and horses of the Eastern Han Dynasty (A.D. 25-220), unearthed in Wuwei.

Upper right: A 34.5-metre-long statue of the Recumbent Buddha in the Great Buddha's Temple in Zhangye. The statue is more than 800 years old and is the biggest of its kind in China.

Lower left: The ancient spring-well into which General Huo Qubing is said to have poured the wine sent by the emperor.

Lower right: Mural of a battle scene in the No. 12 cave of the Mogao Grottoes in Dunhuang. (Opposite)

1—4

Jiayu Mountain, an offshoot of the Qilian Mountains, is snow-clad the year round.

The No. 1 beacon tower at the west end of the Ming Great Wall is located on the banks of the Beida River 15 kilometres south of the main castle of Jiayu Pass. Experts have confirmed that this is the westernmost point of the Ming wall.

Jiayu Pass was the largest fortified castle at the west end of the Ming Great Wall. The square structure has a total space of 35,500 square metres. The main castle lies in an east-west direction. The gates are protected by a wall in front, which is doubled outside the west gate. Corner towers and watchtowers are mounted on the walls of the castle. The various structures are linked by the Great Wall and are combined with the north and south wings of the wall, the forts and the beacon towers to form a watertight defence system. Construction of Jiayu Pass started in 1449 and was completed in 1530. Reconstruction was undertaken during the Qing Dynasty in 1766, 1775 and 1853, but the pass had become thoroughly dilapidated by 1911, the last year of the dynasty. After 1949 it was reconstructed and restored to its shape in the Ming Dynasty. *(Opposite)*

Jiayu Pass

The Great Wall

Sluice gates

Corner terrace

Corner tower   Watchtower

Protective wall

Ramp passage
for horses

Protective wall

Guanghuamen

Rouyuanmen

Stele with the
inscription: "A
Magnificent Pass
of the Empire"

Watchtower

Jiayu Pass at dawn. (Top opposite)

Two gates of Jiayu Pass, the Gate of
Enlightenment and the Gate for Conciliation with
the Remote Peoples, are protected by walls linked
to the wall of the main castle. The picture shows
the Gate of Enlightenment. (Bottom opposite)

A metal plate bearing the character ling, which
means "order." It was a token of authority
permitting one to enter or leave the pass.

The Gate for Conciliation with the Remote Peoples
as viewed from the Gate of Enlightenment.

There is a protruding, raised terrace on each of the four corners of the main castle of Jiayu Pass, with a tower being mounted on each. In addition, there is a protruding terrace in the middle of both the north and south walls of the castle, also with a watchtower resting on each. The picture shows the gatetower of the castle along with a corner tower and a watchtower. (Opposite, top left)

A ramp passage for horses, 2.83 metres wide and 24.73 metres long, is provided at the east gate and the west gate of the main castle of Jiayu Pass, both leading to the gatetower.
(Bottom opposite)

A metal plate for the identification officers and men of the garrison is inscribed with the words: "Every officer or soldier of the garrison is required to carry his plate with him, without which he shall be punished according to law, and anyone who lends it to or borrows it from another person shall be punished alike."

A theatre was built within Jiayu Pass during the Qing Dynasty. It faces the north and is decorated with paintings on the east and west walls.

A plaque hanging on the wall inside the Gate for Conciliation with the Remote Peoples is inscribed with four characters meaning: "The Soul of the Great Wall." (Top right)

Decorations on the tiles of a corner tower of Jiayu Pass. (Bottom right)

長城主宰

The Ming Great Wall terminates at Jiayu Pass, beyond which there is nothing further to the west except ruins of the Han Great Wall.

These are the ruins of Yumen Pass, which was built in the Han period. Located on the Gobi Desert 80 kilometres northwest of the county town of Dunhuang, it was a square castle with a space of over 600 square metres. Yumen means "Gate of Jade." The name has to do with the belief that the famous jade of Hotan in Xinjiang was sent through here to the Central Plains.

This is the site of Yang Pass, 70 kilometres west of Dunhuang County. The heaps of rubble do not look impressive, but buried underneath were many relics of the Han Dynasty. These artifacts have since been excavated by archaeologists.

A scene inside the ruins of Yumen Pass. Both Yumen Pass and Yang Pass were famous in ancient times as important gateways on the Silk Road, which started from the Han capital of Chang'an and split into two roads at Dunhuang. The northern road went through Yumen Pass, and the southern one, through Yang Pass. But the roads beyond the two passes were both hard to negotiate. Thus the names of the two passes became synonymous with a faraway, desolate place. A line from classical Chinese poetry says: "The spring breeze never crosses Yumen Pass." Two other lines read: "Have another cup of wine, won't you? You will meet no more acquaintances once you are outside Yang Pass."

The Great Wall of the Han Dynasty, which reached Lop Nor in Xinjiang 2,000 years ago, has been reduced to ruins by wind and rain, snow and frost. But some parts of it have weathered the storms of the centuries and continue to hold their own in the desert. (Top left)

These young women are selling watermelons at a site which was a thriving market in ancient times.

Though dilapidated, this beacon tower of the Han period seems to retain its dignity.

The Great Wall has lost its value as a defence barrier. But the Chinese will preserve it forever as a marvellous creation of their ancestors and as a symbol of the fortitude of their nation, which will never tolerate foreign domination.

CHRONOLOGY OF THE CONSTRUCTION OF THE GREAT WALL

Period	Wall Built	Delineation or Location	Length (km.)	Dates
Spring and Autumn (770-476 B.C.)	Wall of Qi	South bank of the Yellow River in Pingyin County (western Shandong)-northern slopes of Mount Tai-Yimeng Mountain area-seaboard in Jiao County	Over 500	c. 685-281 B.C.
Warring States (475-221 B.C.)	Wall built under the Jianluo reign of Qin	West bank of Luo River in Shaanxi	Unknown	461-409 B.C.
	Wall built under the reign of King Zhao of Qin	Tao River in Min County (Gansu)-Ningxia-Northern Shaanxi-eastern part of Ordos Plateau in Inner Mongolia	Unknown	c. 287 B.C.
	Wall of Wei, west of the Yellow River	East bank of Luo River in Shaanxi-east bank of Yellow River on Ordos Plateau, called "the wall west of the Yellow River"	About 700	361-352 B.C.
	Wall of Zhao	Yu County, Hebei-southern slopes of Yinshan Mountains, Inner Mongolia-Langshankou Pass, also in Inner Mongolia	About 1,000	c. 299 B.C.
	Wall of Yan	Southeastern Inner Mongolia-northern slopes of Yanshan Mountains-Liaodong	About 1,000	c. 311-279 B.C.
Qin Dynasty (221-207 B.C.)	The Great Wall of Qin	Upper reaches of Tao River Gansu-banks of the Yellow River-northern slopes of Yinshan Mountains-Liaodong, called the 10,000-*li* wall of Qin	5,000	214 B.C.
Western Han Dynasty (206 B.C.-A.D. 24)	Wall of Han	A reinforced version of the wall of Qin, with deviation to the north or south at certain points all the way to Liaodong	5,000	205-127 B.C.
	Wall West of the Yellow River	Lanzhou, Gansu-Yumen Pass-Lop Nor in Xinjiang	1,250	121-101 B.C.
	Guanglu Castle in central Inner Mongolia	Wuchuan County, Inner Mongolia-Urad Rear Banner, also in Inner Mongolia-People's Republic of Mongolia	About 1,000	102 B.C.
	Juyan Castle in northwestern Inner Mongolia	Jiayu Mountain, Gansu-Ejun Banner, Inner Mongolia-People's Republic of Mongolia	About 750	102 B.C.
Northern Wei (386-534)	Wall of Northern Wei	Chicheng, Hebei-Urad Banners, Inner Mongolia	1,000	A.D. 423
Northern Qi (550-577)	Wall of Northern Qi	Lüliang Mountain, Shanxi-Hengshan Mountains-Yanshan Mountains-Juyong Pass near Beijing	About 1,500	552-565
Sui Dynasty (581-618)	Wall of Sui	Yellow River Bend in Ningxia-Inner Mongolia-Shanxi-Hebei-coast of the Bohai Sea, where Yu Pass was built	About 1,500	581-608

Liao Dynasty (916-1125)	Wall of Liao and ditches	Present-day Heilongjiang and Jilin, characterized by ditches in front of the wall	About 1,000	From 908, before inauguration of the dynasty, to 1058
Jin (Jurchen) Dynasty (1115-1234)	Ditches of Jin	Morin Dawa Banner in Hulun Bair League (Inner Mongolia)-southwestern slopes of Greater Hinggan Mountains-northern slopes of Yanshan Mountains-western slopes of Yinshan Mountains, also characterized by ditches in front of the wall	5,000	1200
Ming Dynasty (1368-1644)	The Great Wall of Ming	Yalu River in Liaoning-Hebei-Shanxi-Inner Mongolia-Shaanxi-Ningxia-Jiayu Pass in Gansu	7,300	1368-1644

Index

Liao Dynasty (916-1125)	Wall of Liao and ditches	Present-day Heilongjiang and Jilin, characterized by ditches in front of the wall	About 1,000	From 908, before inauguration of the dynasty, to 1058
Jin (Jurchen) Dynasty (1115-1234)	Ditches of Jin	Morin Dawa Banner in Hulun Bair League (Inner Mongolia)-southwestern slopes of Greater Hinggan Mountains-northern slopes of Yanshan Mountains-western slopes of Yinshan Mountains, also characterized by ditches in front of the wall	5,000	1200
Ming Dynasty (1368-1644)	The Great Wall of Ming	Yalu River in Liaoning-Hebei-Shanxi-Inner Mongolia-Shaanxi-Ningxia-Jiayu Pass in Gansu	7,300	1368-1644

Index